WAR, PEACE, AND THE WOMEN'S INSTITUTE
IN NORTH WALES

By the same author:

Votes for Women

War, Peace, and the Women's Institute
in North Wales

Barbara Lawson-Reay

First published in 2020

© Barbara Lawson-Reay / Gwasg Carreg Gwalch

ISBN: 978-1-84527-732-1

Cover design: Eleri Owen

Published by Gwasg Carreg Gwalch,
12 Iard yr Orsaf, Llanrwst, Wales LL26 0EH
tel: 01492 642031
email: books@carreg-gwalch.cymru
website: www.carreg-gwalch.cymru

This book is for:
The members of the Women's Institute – past and present,
for whom I have the greatest admiration and respect.

and

my husband, John
with gratitude for his patience!

Contents

Notes:

Double-barrelled Surnames: in the Biographies and Index double-barrelled names will be found under the second name.

Place names: I have used the version from the earliest newspaper report, and kept the same version throughout to avoid confusion.

Frequently used abbreviations:

AOS	Agricultural Organisation Society
ASL	Anti-Suffrage League
BOAF	Board of Agriculture and Fisheries
DFP	Denbighshire Free Press
ILP	Independent Labour Party
NFWI	National Federation of Women's Institutes
NLOWS	National League Opposing Women's Suffrage
NUWSS	National Union of Women's Suffrage Societies: law-abiding Suffragists
NWUWI	North Wales Union of Women's Institutes
NWWPC	North Wales Women's Peace Council
SWH	Scottish Women's Hospitals (for service abroad)
QM's	Queen Mary's (Needlework Guild)
UC	University College
UCNW	Univeristy College North Wales, Bangor
WFL	Women's Freedom League
WILPF	Women's International League for Peace and Freedom
WLWC&NW	West Lancashire, West Cheshire & North Wales (NUWSS)
WSPU	Women's Social and Political Union: militant Suffragettes
WI	Women's Institute

Conversion rates:
Average weekly wage for an agricultural labourer working a
fifty-five hour week:
1905 15/-
1910 15/-
1920 16/9d
1925 £1-8/- - £2-2/-

Approximate values in 2019

£	1910	1915	1920	1925
1	78	58	29	41
5	390	294	145	205
10	781	589	290	410
25	1,954	1,474	726	1,026
50	3,908	2,949	1,452	2,052
100	7,871	5,899	2,905	4,105
500	39,086	29,496	14,528	20,529
1,000	78,172	58,922	29,057	41,058

Introduction

My first book *Votes for Women*, looked at the Suffragist's campaign for the vote in North-West Wales from the formation of the first cell of the National Union of Women's Suffrage Societies (NUWSS) in Wales – in Llandudno in 1907, and its spread along the coast in both directions, up to the outbreak of WW1. At that time the NUWSS and the Women's Social and Political Union (WSPU) were asked to give up their political work to support the war effort. This they did wholeheartedly, but never doubted that when the war was over, they would resume campaigning for the vote.

It was never my intention to write a second book, until I discovered that Llangollen NUWSS continued to meet throughout WW1 whilst still supporting the war effort; and furthermore, that the minutes of those meetings still exist.

This book does not set out to comment on the political situation in the eras covered; but simply to bring together descriptions of some of the activities of the North-East Wales and Llangollen Suffragists; Netley and Scottish Women's Hospitals nurses, doctors and patients; Llanfairpwll Women's Institute members; and the men and women who joined the 1926 Welsh Peace Pilgrimage – linked down the years by their desire for equality, justice, compassion, education and peace.

Wherever possible accounts are included verbatim, but due to the early 20th century reporter's tendency never to use one word where ten would do, it has been necessary to summarise many reports whilst retaining the vernacular. I have often wondered whether reporters were paid by the column inch!

Biographies are included at the end of each section.

Section 1

Suffrage Activities in North-East Wales

Reports of the campaign for women's suffrage in North-East Wales are extremely scarce, probably partly due to newspapers of the day being unwilling to encourage those who took part by giving them publicity. Accounts which I have been able to find are recorded here, to provide a background to Section 2 concerning the Llangollen Suffragists.

1906

Around this time a Mr. J. Williams was a reporter for *The Herald*, which he explained was a Labour leaning paper circulating in Johnstown, Pen-y-cae, Ponkey (Ponciau), Rhos(llannerchrugog) and Ruabon; and some of his reminiscences (written in the 1930's) are preserved in the Denbighshire Archives. He explained that it was through the Independent Labour Party (ILP) holding meetings on every street corner in east Denbighshire that they succeeded in getting a fairly good circulation for *The Herald*.

> Seeing the success of the ILP, which until this time had been the only champion of women's suffrage, the Tories started to hold their own meetings. And because women's suffrage was the topic of the day, prominent women speakers who were not necessarily Tories were brought in to address these gatherings, thus trying to

convince those who attended, that voting Tory was their only hope of enfranchisement. Often the women who came to speak on the Tory platforms had no idea what they were being used for until after they had spoken, and it was too late to make it clear that they were in fact, ILP supporters! A very well known ILP supporter who frequently wrote to *The Herald* concerning women's suffrage was Miss Margaret MacDougall and she, to the surprise of the ILP, was engaged by the Tories to speak at an outdoor meeting at Johnstown. Money was spent like water in advertising the meeting. Huge posters were displayed, handbills were distributed and the bellman* was instructed to go to every nook and corner of the rural district. In fact for some days before the meeting took place, the general talk was of the political treat to come. Knowing that there would be an enormous crowd, we, as members of the ILP got together, and discussed the advisability of holding a meeting after theirs – for the purpose of exposing the tactics of the Tory party. Having agreed upon this, we made every preparation for the great day. A special rostrum was to be brought from Wrexham and we arranged for as many ILP members as possible to turn up at the appointed time. I shall never forget how the women turned up, all curious to see and hear Miss MacDougall. Some women arrived with children in their arms, some as if they had left their work half done, some dowdily and some respectably dressed. Every type of village life – respectable and otherwise congregated together with the expectation of a possible row, as much as to hear the speaker! The few policemen present had their work cut out and an anxious time awaited them. At 7 o'clock on a beautiful summer night, the biggest and most expectant crowd that Johnstown had ever seen gathered together. To everyone's disappointment (but to our secret delight) a rumour went around that the lady had not turned up.

On a lorry decorated with flowers sat the chairman, a Conservative working man, and on each side of him sat colleagues. Time was going on but no lady appeared. Their disappointment was evident – their faces showed it, and to cap it all, not a man on the lorry or in the crowd felt they could make a speech. All the chairman had intended to do was introduce the lady speaker. 7.15 and neither the lady nor a substitute had arrived. One can imagine the joy and delight of the ILP boys who were itching for the opportunity to get on the lorry and address the crowd, which was by now growing more and more restless, and someone shouted for a speech from the chairman. Eventually the Conservative agent climbed onto the lorry: not to make a speech, but to say that he had received a wire that the lady speaker had been delayed on the way and it was unlikely that she would be able to attend the meeting. The chairman then declared how disappointed they were and made a humble apology for letting down the crowd ...

*Town crier

Frustratingly, this is where Mr. Williams' report ends. Presumably the ILP members took full advantage of the opportunity which had presented itself!

Mr. Williams' other report concerns a meeting held in Wrexham on a Sunday night:

Wrexham, being anything but Welsh in sentiment, did at least have a smattering of Sabbatarian feeling. Resentment was expressed against Sunday outdoor meetings and consequently ILP members hesitated to take part.

Mr. Williams was persuaded to preside at this meeting on the grounds that because he did not live in Ponciau, he would be less likely than a native of the district to be ostracised for disrespecting the Sabbath. Mr. Williams duly prepared his ten minutes speech and learned it off by heart. He then went on to describe the meeting:

> It was at the end of September and the days were shortening. I appeared, rather on the nervous side, perched on a wagon at the far end of Brook Street alongside this beautiful young woman. We were amongst a type who were [*sic*] not too courteous with their language, and I had particularly noticed a number of men, roughly clad, of the street corner type, who looked as if they'd have felt more comfortable in a boozing den than at a political meeting. In fact I was aware that two or three of them were in the habit of going about disturbing our meetings to gain favour with the wealthy enemy* which meant monetary tips and consequently more beer! They called us red – the only thing red about them was their noses!
>
> My speech was printed indelibly on my brain and I delivered it from A to Z, nothing could stop me – even the biggest of the opponents throwing a rotten pear which unfortunately for me did not miss its target, landing in my left ear, bursting and trickling down inside my clean collar, like an icicle on my bare skin. Concluding, I called upon Miss Christabel Pankhurst to speak and stepped off the lorry, carelessly brushing away with my hand the remains of the rotten pear and smiling in the spirit of turning the other cheek.
>
> The lady delivered her speech in fine style, the interjections from the crowd proving like water off a duck's back. Her motherly advice to the ignorant and

smarting retorts to the abusive kept the huge audience extremely interested. She had been speaking for three quarters of an hour and in the words of the poet:

> The shades of night were falling

enabling the bullying element to seek their prey un-noticed, and they gathered around me bent upon doing damage as soon as Miss Pankhurst wound up her speech. As her beautiful peroration drew to a close I

Christabel Pankhurst

realised I was in for a pair of black eyes to take home – and on a Sunday night too! But having been trained in boxing as a boy, I landed a punch on the big fellow laying him out full length on the ground, and took to my heels up Bridge Street closely followed by his allies, their language renting the air!
*Conservatives

Mr. Williams told how he had turned into Tenter's Square and hidden in a rag and bone store. The gang rambled about trying to locate his whereabouts but eventually gave up. Breathing a prayer of thanks for his safety, he extricated himself from the evil-smelling store and caught a tramcar home. At this point, it suddenly crossed Mr. Williams' mind that he did not know what had happened to Miss Pankhurst and he wondered how he could get back to Wrexham to find out.

An article in *The Wrexham Leader* dated 29 October 2014 – more than a hundred years after this event, described what happened when Christabel Pankhurst came to Wrexham – possibly on this occasion. Mr. Mabon ap Gwynfor explained that he had discovered his great-grandfather, Dan Thomas' diaries which contained an account of an incident involving Miss Pankhurst. He has translated it from the original Welsh and I am very grateful for his permission to include it here.

Mr. Thomas knew that Christabel Pankhurst was due to talk at Rhos about women's rights. A friend of his, Paddy Miller (an Irishman), was tipped off that she was not likely to receive a warm welcome and suggested that they should go and protect her. Dan and some other friends asked what half-a-dozen of them could do against a crowd, but Paddy was convinced that numbers were not important. They went up to Ponciau Banks and found a huge crowd being whipped up into a frenzy by a male speaker. Dan explained to Paddy (who could not speak Welsh), what was going on. Miss Pankhurst then approached the speaker and gave him a right rollicking, at which point another man raised his fist and it was not clear whether he intended to strike her, but he had previously shouted that if the Suffragette did not agree to leave by fair means she would have to be removed by violence.

Dan and Paddy, together with another friend, decided enough was enough. They ran up, Paddy grabbed the man's arm, and Dan and the other friend took Miss Pankhurst's arms and ran with her down the hill towards Johnstown. They found a tavern, ran inside and locked the door, pursued by an angry mob. Dan and his friend stood making rude gestures through the window whilst Paddy led Miss Pankhurst outside to safety.

Later they met up for a meal at The Wynnstay, where

Miss Pankhurst thanked them and they had a brilliant conversation. Dan said it was one of the most interesting experiences of his life thus far:

Who could not admire the boldness of this girl?

He added that her visit had awakened the imagination of himself and his friends. Looking back, Dan said the way they escaped seemed incredible, but he thought the suddenness and nature of their behaviour was the explanation, and that credit must go to Paddy for his daring.

1907
March
On 15 March Margaret Hill B.Sc. wrote to the Editor of *The Llangollen Advertiser* to ask him to publicise the work of The Women's Franchise Declaration Committee. She explained that the object was to collect the signatures of all British subjects who desired that women should vote in parliamentary elections on the same terms as men. The Prime Minister had told them that what they had to do was convince the country that women really did desire the vote. Experience had shown that their numerous petitions had received no attention whatsoever. This therefore was not a petition but a declaration; and when sufficient names had been collected it would be presented to the government. To date, upwards of 30,000 signatures had been appended. Mrs. Hill did not think it would be possible for the government to continue to ignore their demand. She indicated that she would be at home, at 2 Bodwen Villas, Llangollen, to receive further signatures on Thursdays 6-8 pm.
July
It was mentioned in *The Caernarfon & Denbigh Herald* that

Miss Annie Kenney, a Suffragette who had suffered several periods of imprisonment, had spoken at Llangollen.

1908
October
The Denbighshire Free Press (DFP) contained a rather sarcastic report that Suffragetism had invaded the ancient borough of Ruthin. This was a surprise to the DFP staff as they had always looked upon the young ladies of the town as being of the most modest, staid and retiring nature. Anyway, a petition praying the Home Secretary to place Suffragette leaders in Division A* had been taken around the town by the Misses Dawson, Galloway and Morgan, asking for signatures. Local ladies were evidently coming to the fore in matters political.
*Being placed in Division A: political prisoners, meant that the women were not regarded as common criminals. However, it did not prevent them being force fed if they went on hunger strike.
November
A *DFP* reporter noted that St. Asaph's Anti-Suffrage League's (ASL's) petition against the granting of the franchise to women, had been extensively signed by those most interested in the subject.

1909
March
Details of a most interesting debate were published in the *The DFP*. It had taken place at Ruthin Conservative Club on the subject of whether women should have the vote. Unfortunately the women were not allowed to speak for themselves, but were ably represented by Mr. Hodgson, whilst Mr. E.W. Davies spoke against. However, Mr. Hodgson won for the ladies, and the *DFP* reporter

considered that the Conservative men's reputation for chivalry was vindicated!

April

The Llangollen Advertiser contained a report that a public meeting had been held in the Clubroom of The Grapes Hotel, to hear addresses on the subject of Votes for Women. It was considered that the gathering was thoroughly representative with members of both political parties present and it was orderly throughout.

The Grapes Hotel where Llangollen Suffragists first met in April 1909

Miss Beatrice Stewart (Llangollen NUWSS Secretary), who had taken a prominent part in organising the event presided. She was joined on the platform by Mr. Walter Lyon Blease, a Liverpool Barrister. Miss Stewart opened by saying that they had come to hear an address on a subject of vital importance to the nation and she hoped that after it had been delivered, anyone who wished to ask questions would do so.

Miss Stewart continued that the enfranchisement of women concerned Conservatives, Liberals and Socialists alike; and also all those women who professed to take no interest in politics. Women claimed the vote on the grounds of justice: no taxation without representation was a watchword of the British constitution. When women fulfilled the voter's qualifications, justice demanded that they should enjoy the same privileges as men. Legislation which affected men and women ought only to be brought about by the co-operation of both sexes. It was the duty of women to demand the vote, through the exercise of which alone, they could ensure that their interests would be properly looked after.

Miss Stewart questioned what were women's interests? Some legislation, such as taxation, affected both sexes equally. But some affected once sex more than the other, and she would say that Children's Bills, the Midwives' Act and the Bill for the Registration of Nurses, to name but a few, affected women far more than men. All that made for the health of the nation, both physical and moral, concerned the Suffragists. It was not for themselves alone but for the race, that they were asking to be allowed to vote.

Miss Stewart added that she wished to correct a misapprehension which she feared had arisen in the minds of at least a few. Some people did not understand what all the present agitation was about; they thought that women were trying to obtain seats in parliament. She stressed that she wished it to be clearly understood that their demand was for the extension of the franchise – the right for women to vote on the same terms as extended to men. The women of Australia and New Zealand already had the vote, but did not sit in the Colonial Parliament.

The demand for women's suffrage in Britain had been going on for forty-four years. For forty years Suffragists had employed constitutional, ladylike methods, but these did not get the cause very far forward. For the last four years Suffragettes had employed militant tactics, unconstitutional and unladylike – but very manlike! And they had got the cause much further forward. Miss Stewart then explained that all who wanted women to have the vote were Suffragists but those who were trying to obtain it by militancy were Suffragettes: members of the Women's Social and Political Union (WSPU). They were the ones doing the disagreeable work, the ones getting sent to prison. Some people believed the Suffragettes had done the cause a great deal of harm – that remained to be seen. They had revived the ardour of the old-fashioned, constitutional, ladylike societies, and called into being several new societies: the Actresses League for Women's Suffrage, The Conservative and Unionist Women's Society, The Men's League for Women's Suffrage and indeed, the Anti-Suffrage Societies. Miss Stewart observed that the Anti's were very useful to the Suffragists – although they did not know it. They ensured that throughout the length and breadth of the land the subject was being discussed in public meetings, drawing room meetings and by means of that very educational pastime, debate. [*applause*].

Mr. Blease commented that opponents of women's suffrage made two mistakes. Firstly, that the movement was an isolated movement – it was not. It was part of a far greater movement that had been going on for many years in many countries, and had opened the universities, professions and public affairs to women. Secondly, that militant Suffragettes were shrieking viragos – they were not. Many of them were women of culture and refinement and many were of great intellectual attainment. All were animated by their deliberate abandonment of self for a cause. This was what brought revolutions to a successful issue. They recognised that there was one thing greater than law and order, than the control of governments, than life itself – and that thing was liberty. They were told that the tree of liberty was watered with the blood of martyrs. To date no women had shed blood, though many were ready to do even that. But they had shed many tears – the tears of those who had sacrificed their professional prospects, the consolations of home and friendship; and faced the great humiliation of imprisonment not knowing exactly what distress of mind and body would have to be borne. Under those tears the tree of liberty grew straight and strong. [*applause*].

Mr. Blease continued that the same arguments applied to the enfranchisement of women as men. How would Welshmen like to be deprived of their MP's, and told that they were sufficiently represented by MP's chosen by the English? It was claimed that women did not want the vote – but if a substantial number of women demanded it, then they ought to have it. No-one proposed to thrust a burden upon women against their will. The franchise would be a right, and no woman need exercise it unless she wished to do so. Because some did not want it, why should they all be deprived of it? Regarding war, it was true that women could not fight; but many men could not fight and many who could, did not fight – but they had votes. It was not the women's fault they could not fight, why then should they be denied the right to which they were entitled on other grounds? The best argument in favour of the enfranchisement of women was the benefit it would produce for all society. The great questions were those of social reform, upon which the experience and wisdom of women were of special value. The harvest was great and the labourers desperately few. They could not afford to reject the proffered help of women in building up the England of the future [*applause*].

Also in April, it was stated in *The Rhyl Journal* that the National League Opposing Women's Suffrage (NLOWS) had held their first meeting in the area. It had been chaired by Col. Cornwallis-West, Lord Lieutenant of Denbighshire, who claimed that it was discontented married women who were agitating for the vote, and lately upsetting the whole country! The meeting was well attended by the gentry of Denbighshire and Flintshire and Mrs. Cornwallis-West became president of Rhyl NLOWS.

June

The North Wales Express contained a report that the NUWSS had held an open meeting in Llangollen. The speakers were Mr. Blease, Miss Helga Gill (Welsh NUWSS Organiser), Dr. Alice Stewart-Ker, a Birkenhead GP and Mrs. Cobden-Sanderson (WSPU/Women's Freedom League) (WFL). Coming so soon after the interruption of the London Eisteddfod by Suffragettes, the timing of the Llangollen meeting was judged ill-chosen. Young men marched into Llangollen from Cefn, Ruabon and other parts of the locality, singing *Hen Wlad fy Nhadau* (*Land of our Fathers*) and intending to get a bit of their own back. No speaker was allowed to proceed without uproar:

who disturbed the Eisteddfod?

was a frequent cry. Obviously the speakers truthfully denied that the NUWSS had anything to do with the interruption of the Eisteddfod, but the young men were not convinced.

Despite the continued racket, the reporter managed to give an account of an unusual message from Mrs. Cobden-Sanderson, who said that the Welsh were Celts and Celts had imagination. If you had imagination it followed that you were not prejudiced. Prime Minister Asquith had described himself as Anglo-Saxon. Everyone knew that the Anglo-

Saxons had no imagination and Asquith was definitely prejudiced! She appealed to all the chivalrous Welshmen present that night to use their imaginations – to try to understand why women wanted the vote, and to help them get it. At the close of the meeting only twelve people voted in favour of votes for women – but no-one actually voted against. The meeting closed, still in pandemonium with cheers for popular Welsh poiticians and more Welsh songs.

August

On 21 August an item in *The DFP* headlined the publication of the ASL's first Annual Report:

NO VOTES FOR WOMEN – ANTI-SUFFRAGISTS PUT
THE BRAKE ON

The reporter went on to say that the league congratulated itself on having achieved its objective by exerting a distinct check on the women's suffrage movement.

September

The Suffragist's *The Common Cause* magazine described Miss Helga Gill's return to Wales. Shortly after arriving she had one of the calamities itinerant organisers accepted as part of daily life – when her tethered horse almost strangled itself. An observer with a literary turn of phrase commented that:

> had it not been possible to cut the cord at once, the unfortunate rosinante* would now have been cropping celestial food in the Elysian Fields.
> * emaciated and decrepit old horse

The police banned meetings at Wrexham and Ruabon on the grounds that these mining towns were terribly rough and strongholds of Liberalism. At Trefor near Llangollen an attempted meeting was abandoned due to gangs of roughs who gathered in force. Placards were torn to ribands [*sic*], brickbats were collected and the uncontrolled excitement of the whole populace was enormous. Hostility was also demonstrated in Llangollen itself and so the women changed their tactics. Instead of trying to hold meetings immediately they arrived; they started to distribute literature first – some of it in Welsh, house to house, shop to shop and mill to mill. The Suffragists made a real attempt to get to know the local people, in the hope they would then be eager to hear what they – the Suffragists, had to say. Unfortunately even this strategy did not work at Bala where the Suffragist's meeting was broken up by an unruly crowd, and the speakers had to be escorted away by police. But Welsh speaker, Miss Magdalen Morgan, a teacher from South Wales, fared a lot better at Corwen, the surrounding area, and as far as Dolgellau.

Helga Gill complained that everywhere they went they were greeted with the question:

Why did you break up our (London) Eisteddfod?

and it was difficult to convince people that they (the NUWSS) had not done so – the WSPU had.

November

The DFP contained a report that Denbigh Literary Society had debated the burning question of whether the parliamentary franchise should be granted to women. Mr. R.B. Searell presided, the case for was put by Mr. Askew and against by Mr. Cecil Owen.

Mr. Askew explained that it was no part of his brief to take into account how women had gone about seeking the franchise, simply to consider the principle. If women's brains were smaller than men's, then their quality was demonstrated by famous women in the realms of art, literature, science and business. Opponents would argue that women's place was in the home and that they should not take part in political life. But even business women were not allowed to vote, although their male employees were – where was the justice in that?

Mr. Owen replied that women did not have an absolute right to vote, it was not expedient to give them the vote and furthermore, women themselves did not want the vote. The main qualification for men was that they paid taxes and although some women did, they lacked equality with men in every other way – and undoubtedly physically and intellectually. Men provided the wherewithal and women should look after the home.

Various other men gave their opinions and the Literary Society members decided against giving the vote to women by twenty-four votes to fourteen.

1910
September
In mid-September it was reported in *The DFP* that the NUWSS had held their first Denbigh meeting in the Town Hall. Preparations were hurriedly made and the ladies' method of announcing their arrival was novel and yet somewhat incomplete. People were surprised to see details of the meeting chalked on the pavements around the hall, but many who might otherwise have attended, unfortunately knew nothing about it. Further, had the Suffragists consulted friends familiar with the town, they might have avoided the disturbance which made it impossible for them to speak in comfort; and very difficult for them to make themselves heard at all. The bulk of the audience was at least mildly interested in hearing the speaker's views; but the gallery was packed with boys who

The Town Hall where Denbigh Suffragists first met in September 1910

caused a continual disturbance by shouting, singing and the employment of unmusical instruments of every kind! Nine or ten men scattered through the gallery would have had no difficulty in keeping these boys quiet or turning them out of the hall. Most of them should have been at home in bed before the meeting even began. It was only fair to the speakers to say that they bore the noisy interruptions with perfect good humour, in some cases even turning it to their own advantage.

The Chairwoman, Miss Gimingham, opened the meeting by saying they were all aware that it had been arranged at very short notice and were therefore grateful to have such a splendid attendance! She was immediately drowned out by a bugle and whistles. She persisted that she wanted to tell them about the NUWSS, but was interrupted by more shouting and singing from the gallery. During a pause on the part of the lusty opposition, the speaker complained that it was not at all fair of them to disturb her as they were doing – they had had plenty of time to entertain the audience before the meeting started. This remark was greeted with more hoots of derision, but they eventually subsided sufficiently for Miss Gimingham to explain that they belonged to no political party; and had only one object in view – to obtain votes for women. But not for all women – only for women who were properly qualified to have a vote. It was extraordinary that this was the first meeting to be held in Denbigh, because both past and present MP's for the borough were strongly in favour of women's enfranchisement. She could also have cited the fact that, as early as 1863 a Denbigh resident, Susannah Gee, had signed a petition calling for women's suffrage.

Miss Gimingham then introduced Miss Chrystal MacMillan whom, she said, had given a five hours speech to the House of Lords. Predictably, there were shouts about her not giving a five hours speech that night and further boos and whistles. Miss Macmillan started out by complimenting the audience on their responsiveness, before being drowned out. Mr. E.J. Roberts, the schoolmaster, appealed for the ladies to be given a fair hearing, but to no avail. Miss MacMillan continued that the people who broke the law – the Suffragettes, and people who kept the law – the Suffragists, both had a right to take part in making the law in the first place. She commented that she had recently watched only men going into a polling station, but the tax office was in the same building and both men and women entered that. If women paid tax they should be allowed to vote on the same terms as men. Currently only paupers, criminals, lunatics – and women were disqualified! But women were perfectly capable of making their own decisions and she cited Nurse Florence Nightingale as an example, which elicited cheers from the gallery. At this point the noise was so deafening that Miss

Gimingham, Mr. Roberts and a Miss Lamond all appealed for quiet. But although Miss MacMillan continued, it was very difficult to hear all she had to say – mainly concerning the laws which affected women.

Miss Lamond then stated that eight million men were already qualified to vote. If women got the vote only about one and a half million of them would qualify to start with, but they (the Suffragists) were willing to accept this as an instalment, and work hard to increase the number. At this point someone threw a bucket of cold water over some of the boys in the gallery – who retaliated by throwing a bench through a window. The meeting descended into chaos, but once order was restored it closed with a collection and enrolment of those wishing to support the NUWSS in Denbigh.

The reporter seemed quite sympathetic towards the Suffragists, saying that is was very unfair that they had been unable to get their message across due to being confused with the militant Suffragettes. He added that the rowdy boys would not have dared interrupt a political meeting addressed by a male. The Editor apologised for being unable to provide a full summary, partly due to the reporter being unable to hear all the speeches and partly because some of the interruptions were unfit for publication!

October

The DFP contained a report that on Wednesday 22 October Miss Ciceley Leadley-Brown from Liverpool and Mrs. Selina Cooper from Nelson had spoken on the subject of women's suffrage at a meeting in The Square at Ruthin, and had been very well received.

A second women's suffrage meeting had been held in Denbigh Town Hall addressed by these same two women. Entrance was by ticket only, and the audience was generally very orderly; despite the presence at the back of the hall of a few rowdy youths. Miss Leadley-Brown opened the meeting by explaining that the first women to get the vote would be those already qualified to take part in municipal elections. She continued that women did not look upon the campaign for enfranchisement as a battle between themselves and men – they appreciated the fact that many men supported them. Women in America, Australia and New Zealand already had the vote, so why should Britain lag behind? What women wanted was equality – and not just in voting rights, but in pay too. It was regarded as acceptable that men earned higher wages because they had families to support, but many women had aged parents to support and did not receive the same consideration.

Mrs. Cooper then spoke, but unlike Miss Leadley-Brown, did suffer from some rowdyism from the youths at the back of the hall. Mrs. Cooper spoke about the need for equal pay for identical work and the fact that taxation must go hand in hand with representation.

Miss Leadley-Brown then appealed to any ladies present to join the newly formed Denbigh branch of the NUWSS and several ladies signed up.

December

An item in *The Wrexham Advertiser* informed readers that Miss Rachel Barrett, the Welsh WSPU Organiser, was holding regular meetings in Denbigh, Ruthin and Wrexham with a view to returning a candidate at the next election who supported women's enfranchisement. The Conservative candidate, William Ormesby-Gore, wisely towed the pro-women's suffrage line and was rewarded by winning the Denbigh Boroughs seat by just nine votes.

1911

March

In an article in *The Common Cause* Llangollen was portrayed as:

a little suffrage oasis in the midst of a desert of indifference.

This was re-printed in *The Llangollen Advertiser*

The NUWSS urged groups to lobby public bodies, and Wrexham NUWSS supporters succeeded in persuading the town's council to support the latest Suffrage Bill.

1912
February
Mrs. Emmeline Pankhurst's visit to Wrexham was covered by a *Wrexham Advertisr* reporter. She spoke at a well attended meeting at the Drill Hall and moved a resolution condemning the proposal to introduce a Suffrage Bill confined to men; and calling upon the government to bring in a measure giving equal voting rights to women. This was passed, but with a few dissensions.

August
Towards the end of the month *The Common Cause* contained a report that the West.Lancashire, West Cheshire and North Wales NUWSS caravan (which was actually a parcels delivery van with a white tarpaulin cover) was touring/had toured Cheshire and Flintshire. Meetings were held at Buckley, Caergwrle, Flint, Hawarden (where Helen Gladstone, daughter of four times Prime Minister Gladstone, chaired the meeting), Mold and Northop; but no further societies were formed as a result of this campaign.

September
This month an incident occurred claimed by *The Western Mail* reporter to have been the most serious outside London. Actress, Kitty Marion, attended the National Eisteddfod of Wales at Wrexham, seat 338, row 11, block C, price 5/- and heckled Mr. Lloyd-George. The reporter continued:

Kitty Marion at the National Eisteddfod, Wrexham, 1912

It was outside the pavilion that the worst scenes of retaliation took place. The police were helpless to protect their charges from the infuriated mass, which had developed into a mob outside the doors. Each of the women were smacked on the face, each one lost her hat, had bundles of hair torn ruthlessly from their roots and each one suffered indignities. Blood flowed from the face of one woman and the scalps of all of them bled owing to the uprooting of hair, and a credible eye-witness gave an account of a knife being used against one of the women. It was seen to gleam in the sun and descend upon the breast of a woman but happily the cut was not serious. The police were helpless and the assailant was not arrested. The coats, dresses and blouses of the five women were torn more or less badly and indeed one woman was almost stripped of her upper garments and she presented a most sorry spectacle. Miss Marion was not arrested on this occasion.

It was recounted in a Liberal Party publication that Wrexham Trophies – strips of material torn from the women's clothing, were sent as keepsakes to eminent men who had attended the Eisteddfod.

After the disruption at the Eisteddfod, Mrs. Gladstone Solomon took full advantage of the situation by promoting the need for branches of the ASL:

> wherever the public had had the misfortune to experience militant suffragism and resultant anarchy.

It is interesting that, very shortly after the incident at Wrexham, Mr. Lloyd George's opening of a new Village Hall at his home, Llanystumdwy, was again interrupted by Suffragettes. It is recorded in an article in *The Journal of Liberal Democratic History 34/35 Summer 2002* by Dr. Graham Jones that both the *Daily Mirror* and *Daily Telegraph* dated 23 September 1912 carried reports as follows:

> It was further reported that the shirts of the protesting women were cut up and distributed among the crowd as souvenirs of this momentous occasion.

In addition it was claimed that the Suffragettes had had handfuls of their hair torn out – although this was refuted by Evan William Evans, journalist and owner of a Dolgellau printing office. He had seen one of the women's hats come off – and handfuls of hair with it. His friend had picked up the hat and found a considerable quantity of false hair concealed inside – which, when the hat was removed from the wearer's head, did come off in handfuls.

New Zealand's *The Poverty Bay Herald* even contained a report headed *Like Porcupines* which stated that the

Suffragettes had learned a valuable lesson at Wrexham. They had taken the precaution of turning up at Llanystumdwy wearing padded clothes with needles inserted – tips outwards, thus preventing them being man-handled.

1914
February

On Shrove Tuesday Llangollen NUWSS held a Pancake Tea and Cake Sale for the general public, ably organised by Miss Beatrice Stewart. It was very well attended, and once the ladies had enjoyed their pancakes they were introduced to the NUWSS by novel means. Mrs. Greville Stalybrass had secured the use of a gramophone, and proceeded to play short, recorded *speechlets* giving information about the Suffragist's cause. These explained that women wanted the vote to benefit not just themselves, but their families. However well meaning some husbands were, they could not really know how their wives felt and therefore could not vote in women's best interests. And every year, more and more bills which affected women's lives were coming up – so it was only right that women should be consulted on what passed into law.

Section 1a

Denbigh, Ruthin and Wrexham NUWSS
Who was Who

Denbigh supporters:

Mr. E.J. ROBERTS, Schoolmaster

Ruthin supporters:

Miss DAWSON
Miss GALLOWAY
Miss MORGAN

Wrexham officers:

Miss Laura Catherine PRICE, 76 Beechley Road, secretary
Miss Howell-DAVIES, 14 Foster Road, treasurer

Wrexham supporters:

Miss Margaret MacDOUGALL

Section 1b

Visiting Suffragettes, Suffragists and Supporters
Who was Who

Almost inevitably the paths of some of the men and women listed below crossed, therefore I have included only the first account of each event, if more than one was present.

Miss Rachel BARRETT was born in 1875. In 1912 she was appointed editor of *The Suffragette* newspaper. In 1913 she was arrested at the paper's London HQ along with staff, tried for conspiracy, found guilty and sentenced to nine months in Holloway. As a result of going on hunger strike she was released under the Cat and Mouse Act – which allowed sick Suffragettes to be released early; to save the government the embarrassment of having them die in prison. Once the women recovered, they could be re-arrested and re-imprisoned. Later she published *The Suffragette* in Edinburgh.

She was also a WSPU Organiser in Wales. Rachel Barrett died in 1953.

Mr. Walter Lyon BLEASE, was born in 1884 in Liverpool, the son of Walter and Mary Blease. (Mr. Blease Snr. was a chartered accountant and Mrs. Blease, a Poor Law Guardian). Mr. Blease Jnr. was educated in Liverpool, graduated in Law from Liverpool University and was called to the bar in 1906. He then lectured in Law at Liverpool 1910-1915 and 1919-1949. He was the first president of the Liverpool branch of the Men's League for Women's Suffrage, founded in 1908. His book *The Emancipation of English Women*, was published in 1910

In WW1 Mr. Blease served with Red Cross hospital units in Roumania, Russia and Serbia. In 1918 he married Harriott Davies and they had three daughters. In 1936 Mr. Blease was appointed to the British Board of Film Censors and in 1939 would have stood as Liberal candidate for East Toxteth, Liverpool, had not WW2 intervened, meaning that there was no election. He was Liberal candidate for Garston, Liverpool, in 1950 but lost to the Conservatives. He was also chairman of Liverpool Philharmonic Orchestra 1950-51. Walter Lyon Blease died in 1963.

Miss Ciceley Leadley-BROWN, was a Liverpool barrister and in 1918 she is known to have been employed as Welfare Supervisor at a National Projectile Factory.

Mrs. Selina COOPER, (nèe **Coombe**) was born in 1864 in Cornwall, the daughter of Charles and Jane. Charles was a navvy and died when Selina and her brother were very young, leaving them and their mother destitute. Jane and these two youngest children moved to Lancashire, where her two older sons were already working.

Selina and her brother

Selina Cooper

soon found work in the local mill. Selina was twelve by this time and therefore a half-timer – spending the other half of the day at school. At thirteen she was able to leave school and work full-time, earning eight shillings for a fifty-six hour week. Her mother, who had severe rheumatism was housebound, but managed to take in dress-making. Eventually Selina had to leave the mill to care for her mother, but when her mother died in 1889, Selina returned to the mill. She joined the Cotton Workers Union but soon realised that this union, representing a high proportion of women, was run exclusively by men. They had no interest in improving the women's terrible working conditions, for example there were no doors on the lavatories. Selina attended classes run by the Women's Co-operative Guild, and read books on history and politics. She also read medical books in the hope of being able to assist fellow workers with medical problems – particularly birth control, as they were unable to afford to consult doctors.

In 1892 she started attending local ILP meetings, attracted by their support of equal rights for women. There she met Robert Cooper, a weaver, who had been sacked from his previous job in the Post Office due to his trade union activities. They married in 1896 and had three children, one of whom died in infancy.

In 1900 Selina Cooper joined the North of England Society for Women's Suffrage. Almost immediately she helped to organise a petition supporting women's suffrage, and by early 1901 nearly 29,500 women working in the Lancashire cotton mills had signed it. She personally collected eight hundred signatures and was chosen as one of the delegates to take the petition to the House of Commons. Next the ILP asked her to stand for election as a Poor Law Guardian, and despite a lot of opposition from local newspapers (no working-class woman had ever stood before), she won. Predictably she was out-voted on many issues but did manage to secure greater freedom of movement for the elderly. Previously husbands and wives had been segregated on entering the Workhouse and not allowed to even see each-other. In 1906 Mrs. Cooper was a founder member of the Nelson and District Suffrage Society. By this time she was in demand nationally as an eloquent and passionate speaker at NUWSS Rallies. In 1910 she was one of four women chosen to speak to the Prime Minister about women's suffrage.

By 1911 she was a full-time NUWSS Organiser and so valuable was she to the National Union that they paid for a housekeeper to look after her husband and children. In 1912 she influenced the NUWSS' strategy of supporting Labour candidates at the forth-coming election. This was not universally popular with members, many of whom were Liberals or Conservatives.

Mrs. Cooper was a pacifist, opposed to conscription and tried to help conscientious objectors. In 1917 she persuaded over a thousand women in Nelson to support a Women's Peace Procession which ended in a riot. Mounted police had to intervene to protect her and a fellow speaker.

After the war – and enfranchisement, the NUWSS tried to persuade the Nelson Labour Party to select Mrs. Cooper as their candidate, but the still male-dominated party refused. However, she was elected to Nelson Town Council and became a magistrate. In the 1930's she campaigned against racism. Selina Cooper died in 1946.

Miss Helga GILL, was a Norwegian who became an NUWSS Organiser for Wales.

Miss C. GIMINGHAM, was described in *The Woman Teacher, 16 Nov 1928* as one of the New Guard (of

Suffragists). The report concerned a Victory Lunch and Reception at Caxton Hall. The event was chaired by Viscountess Rhondda who had been an active Suffragette. Caxton Hall was thought to be a fitting venue, because Suffragettes had set out from the hall on many occasions to fight the battle for freedom. Miss Gimingham commented that:

> Although the victory was due to the Old Guard, the future rests with the New Guard: the vote was not a trophy; but a sword, shield and standard. It must never be said that the New Guard rests on the laurels of the old. The young girl of today knows what she wants and is going to get it.

She added that it was far easier to vote than to make a speech about it.

Annie Kenney

Miss Annie KENNEY, was born in 1879 in Saddleworth, Lancashire, one of the eleven children of Horatio and Ann. At the age of ten, when the family's budget was more than usually tight, she worked for a short period as a half-timer at a local mill and subsequently worked full-time – losing a finger whilst doing so. She hated the way the WSPU publicised this throughout her life. Although poor, her family certainly recognised the value of education. Four of her sisters became teachers, and a brother became Editor of *The Daily Herald* before working as a *Reutters* correspondent in WW1. Annie was the first woman to be elected onto the local committee of her trades union.

Early in 1905 Annie went to an ILP meeting addressed by Christabel Pankhurst and was so impressed that she arranged for Christabel to speak to a group of women mill workers. Annie joined the WSPU and before long was speaking to the mill workers herself. Soon afterwards she left the mill and went to work as a WSPU Organiser in London's East End.

In the late autumn of 1905 Annie went, with Christabel Pankhurst, to a meeting in Manchester Free Trade Hall where Winston Churchill and Sir Edward Grey were the speakers, and boldly stood up and asked:

If you are elected will, you do your best to make women's suffrage a government measure?

After a scuffle the two women were forcibly ejected and charged with obstruction. They refused to pay their fines and were given short prison sentences. They were delighted by the resulting publicity. There followed many more incidents and prison sentences.

In 1907 Annie was moved to Bristol to work as WSPU Organiser there. When Christabel fled to France in 1912 Annie was re-called to London and travelled secretly to Paris every week to receive Christabel's instructions and implement them on her return. She did not agree with the escalation of militancy but would not cross Christabel. In 1913 Annie was charged with incitement to riot and imprisoned for eighteen months. She immediately went on hunger strike and was the first Suffragette to be released under the Cat and Mouse Act. On her release Annie spent a short time in Paris, but with the outbreak of WW1 was instructed to return to England on the grounds that it would not be a good idea to have both WSPU's leaders (Christabel and Annie) in France, should the country be invaded by Germany.

Annie was then sent to the United States – which she hated; and when Christabel arrived to try to encourage America to join the war, Annie managed to persuade Christabel to allow her to return to England. In 1915 Annie was sent to Australia to assist Prime Minister, Billy Hughes (who had been brought up in Llandudno), to try to get a positive response in a referendum on conscription. On her return to England Annie helped Mr. Lloyd George with his campaign to recruit female munitions workers.

After the war and women's enfranchisement Annie helped Christabel with her bid to become MP for Smethwick – but this venture failed. Annie then went to live with a fellow Suffragette. Annie was known to have had a considerable number of lesbian affairs during her time in the WSPU. Whilst on holiday with her sister she met James Taylor, they were married in 1920 and had a son in 1921. Annie lost interest in politics but kept in touch with Christabel for the rest of her life. Annie explained:

> There is a cord between Christabel and me that nothing can break – the cord of love... We started militancy side by side and we stood together until victory was won.

Annie died in 1953. Her ashes were scattered on Saddleworth Moor. In 2018 her statue was unveiled outside Oldham Town Hall.

Dr. Alice Jane Shannan Stewart-KER, was born in 1853 in Banffshire, daughter of the Rev William Turnbull Ker, minister of the Free Church of Scotland, and his wife, Margaret. On leaving school, Alice went to Edinburgh University, but when a campaign to persuade the university to grant medical degrees to women failed, Alice transferred to the King and Queen's College of Physicians of Ireland in Dublin and was awarded her Licentiateship. After further study in Switzerland she worked in Birmingham and as a GP in Leeds, before returning to Edinburgh to take the Royal College of Surgeons examination, which she passed. In 1888 she married her cousin, Edward Stewart-Ker and they moved to Birkenhead. They had two daughters; and a son who died in infancy. As well as running her own practice she worked for other local organisations and lectured on birth control and motherhood. In 1891 these lectures were published as: *Motherhood: A Book for Every Woman*.

In 1893 Dr. Stewart-Ker joined the Birkenhead and Wirral Women's Suffrage Society, and after her husband's death in 1907, her interest in women's suffrage became hugely important to her. She became chair of her local society but increasingly felt they were too moderate and transferred to the WSPU. In March 1912 after taking part in mass stone-throwing at government office windows, she was arrested, imprisoned in Holloway, and forcibly fed. She was released under The Cat and Mouse Act before completing her sentence. She then continued to work as a doctor in Liverpool but was asked to leave one of the hospitals where she had been employed. She advocated pacifism during WW1, and joined the Women's International League for Peace and Freedom (WILPF). Dr. Stewart-Ker died in 1943.

Wilhelmina Hay LAMOND was born in 1883 in Scotland. She later adopted the name **Elizabeth**. She was educated in London, Brussels and at UC London before training as a secretary and accountant. In 1909 she became the organiser for the Edinburgh National Society for Women's Suffrage and campaigned in the Scottish Highlands. In 1910 she became a member of the Executive Committee of the Scottish Federation of Women's Suffrage. In 1911 she married George Frederick Abbott and they had one son.

During WW1 she gave lecture tours in Australia, India and New Zealand, raising £60,000 for Scottish Women's Hospitals (SWH). After the war she joined Chrystal MacMillan in the Open Door and Open Door International projects – campaigning for equal employment opportunities for women. She also worked for forty years for the Association for Moral and Social Hygiene – concerned with the prevention of prostitution and venereal disease. She died in 1957.

Miss Chrystal MacMILLAN, was born in 1882 in Edinburgh, the only daughter (she had eight brothers) of John MacMillan, a wealthy tea merchant. In 1892 she was one of the first women to be admitted to Edinburgh University and gained a BSc. with first-class honours.

In 1902 she joined the NUWSS. The Scottish universities had four MP's elected by their General Councils – which included all graduates. Miss MacMillan therefore decided to establish whether the word *person* used throughout the statute, included women. In 1908

Chrystal MacMillan

she became the first woman to address the House of Lords – advocating that women graduates should be given the vote. Although not at that time a lawyer, she was said to have shown considerable skill in presenting her case – but it was still rejected.

Around 1910 Miss MacMillan moved to London and joined the Executive Committee of the NUWSS. She was also a member of the WFL and in 1913 became vice-president of the International Women's Suffrage Alliance. She also gave evidence to various committees on such matters as unemployment insurance, prostitution and women losing their citizenship when they married non-British nationals.

At an NUWSS Council Meeting early in 1915 Mrs. Millicent Fawcett argued that until the German army had been driven out of France and Belgium, it was akin to treason to talk of peace. All the officers (except the treasurer), and ten members of the National Executive – including Miss MacMillan resigned over the decision not to support the Women's Peace Congress at The Hague. Miss MacMillan attended the conference.

In 1924 she was called to the English Bar:

Her chief aim in life – one might call it her passion, was to give every woman, of every class and nation, the essential protection of justice.

In 1923 she became a founder member of the Open Door Council, and in 1929 a founder member and president of Open Door International. In the 1935 Election she stood as the Liberal candidate for Edinburgh North but was unsuccessful. Miss MacMillan died in 1937 and was buried in the village of Corstorphine near Edinburgh.

Miss Kitty MARION, was born in Germany. Her mother died when she was just two years old. As a teenager, in 1886, she came to England to stay with her aunt to teach herself English, and have dancing lessons – because she was determined to follow a career on the stage. By 1889 she was appearing in pantomime in Glasgow; then toured Britain in the Music Halls – billed as a refined, vocal, comedienne. By 1899 she was appearing in Liverpool in the same show as Vesta Tilley – the famous male impersonator.

Kitty Marion joined the WSPU and then, as soon as it was formed, the Actresses' Franchise League (AFL), selling the Suffragette's *Votes for Women* on the streets and taking part in campaigns. In 1909, after throwing a stone at a building which she knew Mr. Lloyd-George was visiting, she was arrested, went to prison, and whilst on hunger strike was forcibly fed for the first time. She received the WSPU Hunger Strike medal in December, just before embarking on the 1909 pantomime season.

She also took part in the Variety Artists' Federation campaign against theatrical agents – believing some to be white slave traders. This resulted in the agents being required to be licensed.

Kitty continued to support WSPU campaigns, including arson, and continued to be arrested, imprisoned, go on hunger and thirst strike, be forcibly fed, and released under The Cat and Mouse Act. She also continued to appear on stage whenever she was free and well enough to do so.

During WW1 Kitty was threatened with deportation back to Germany, but was allowed to go to the United States instead. She spent the rest of her life promoting birth-control and spending some time in American prisons as a result.

Miss Christabel PANKHURST, was born in 1880 in Old

Trafford, Manchester, the eldest daughter of Richard and Emmeline.

At the 1902 Labour Party Conference her mother tried to persuade members to support female enfranchisement but failed. As a result, Mrs. Pankhrst left the Labour Party and formed the WSPU.

After Christabel's brief period of imprisonment with Annie Kenney, and the new Liberal government of 1906 failing to make any progress towards women's enfranchisement, Christabel became more militant. In 1907 she gained a first-class law degree, but could not pursue a career as a barrister due to being a woman. She then moved to London and was appointed the WSPU's chief organiser. At this time she lived with Frederick and Emmeline Pethick-Lawrence. Christabel was not convinced that the WSPU should be seeking the support of the working-class and concentrated her energy on recruiting more prosperous women, pointing out that without their financial support there would not be a WSPU. It was thought that what Christabel actually wanted was votes for **ladies**! Her mother supported her, but her sisters Adela and Sylvia did not – they wanted the vote for all women.

In the autumn of 1907, seventy-six members of the WSPU, feeling that the organisation was undemocratic and completely dominated by Christabel and her mother, left to form the WFL.

In 1909 Marion Wallace-Dunlop went on hunger-strike and subsequently Christabel advocated this tactic. She also persuaded 116 doctors to sign a letter to the Prime Minister asking him to stop the practice of forcible feeding, and instigated the stone throwing campaign as a means of protest against it.

At the 1910 Election the Liberals lost votes and needed support from Labour. The Conciliation Committee was set up with the support of both Mrs. Fawcett and Mrs. Pankhurst and Suffragette's militancy was temporarily halted. However, after a decent interval, with no sign of a Conciliation Bill being passed, the Suffragettes resumed their militant campaign with a spate of window smashing in Whitehall and Fleet Street. Mrs. Pankhurst was asked to control her members in order to get the bill passed, but she replied she wished she had never heard of:

the abominable Conciliation Bill

and predictably, it was thrown out.

In 1912 the WSPU carried out a shop-window smashing campaign, the Pethick-Lawrences remonstrated with Christabel about this, but she ignored them and banned men, including Mr. Pethick-Lawrence, from membership of the WSPU. Mr. Pethick-Lawrence had financed the legal representation for many Suffragettes facing trial, as well as the publication of *The Suffragette* magazine. The shop-window smashing campaign resulted in many high-profile members leaving the WSPU – believing that militancy was once again damaging the cause. When the government ordered the arrest of the WSPU leaders, Christabel escaped to Paris but Frederick and Emmeline Pethick-Lawrence were arrested, tried, and sentenced to nine months imprisonment. They were also successfully sued for the cost of the damage caused by the WSPU, which all but bankrupted them. But Christabel remained unconcerned and initiated an arson campaign through Annie Kenney.

Once WW1 was declared the government agreed to release all Suffragettes from prison, in return for a cessation of militancy and support for the war effort. Christabel returned from Paris. The title of *The Suffragette* was changed to: *Britannia – for King, for Country, for Freedom* and attacked politicians and military leaders for not doing enough to win the war.

When the vote was won, the WSPU was dis-banded and Christabel and her mother formed The Women's Party, which Christabel stood for at the 1918 election, hoping to represent Smethwick – but she was unsuccessful. In 1921 she and her mother emigrated to Canada where Christabel joined the Seventh Day Adventist sect. They later moved to America, then in 1925 she and her mother set up a tea shop in France with someone else's money and baking skills! This was unsuccessful and they returned to England in 1926. Christabel then joined the Conservatives but was unable to find a winnable seat and blamed women voters for not supporting her. She was awarded the DBE in the 1936 New Year's Honours List. In 1939 she returned to America and continued to lecture and write books on religion, until her death in 1958. She was buried in the Woodlawn Memorial Cemetery, Santa Monica, California.

Emmeline PANKHURST (nèe **Goulden**) was born in 1858 in Manchester and taken to her first suffrage meeting at the age of fourteen by her mother, a passionate feminist. In 1879 Emmeline married Dr. Richard Pankhurst, a lawyer and strong advocate of women's suffrage. They had three daughters: Christabel, Adela and Sylvia, and two sons: Frank and Harry, both of whom pre-deceased Emmeline.

Emmeline Pankhurst, founder, WSPU

After Dr. Pankhurst, who stood as an Independent, was defeated in the 1883 Election, the family moved to London and Mrs. Pankhurst opened a stationers, and an art furniture shop – intended to rival Liberty's, opposite which it was situated. Neither venture was very successful.

In 1893 the family returned to Manchester and Dr. and Mrs. Pankhurst formed a branch of the ILP. At the 1895 Election Dr. Pankhurst stood as an ILP candidate but was again defeated. When he died in 1898 Mrs. Pankhurst was forced to move to a smaller house and take up employment as a registrar of births and deaths. She became increasingly disillusioned with the existing women's suffrage organisations and when, in 1903, she discovered that a Memorial Hall named in her husband's honour would not admit women (bearing in mind that he had always fully supported women's suffrage), she was inspired, together with her daughters, to form the WSPU with the battle cry:

Deeds not Words.

By 1907 the chief registrar had decided that Mrs. Pankhurst's WSPU activities were no longer compatible with her position and informed her of this. With little hesitation Mrs. Pankhurst moved back to London and spent the rest of her life staying in hotels or with her supporters. She was imprisoned on countless occasions but her imperious demeanour seemed to paralyse even the most hardened prison officials and what she wanted, e.g. her watch, books and writing materials, she usually got! Although she did threaten to go on hunger and thirst strike it is not clear whether she was ever forcibly fed. On occasions her own food was brought in, accompanied by half pints of Château Lafite!

Towards the end of 1909 she embarked on her first lecture tour in the US. By this time, her daughters, Adela and Sylvia, were convinced that the sustained campaign of militancy was losing support for the WSPU – but Mrs. Pankhurst and Christabel would have none of it. In fact when Mrs. Pankhurst set out for her third lecture tour in the US, the British Embassy in Washington offered to advise the American government not to allow her to enter the country, if the British government feared the financial support for the WSPU which would result from her engagements, but the offer was declined.

During WW1, at the behest of her erstwhile enemy, Mr. Lloyd George, Emmeline agreed to try to recruit women to work in munitions – on the understanding that they would be paid at the same rate as men.

Mrs. Pankhurst died in 1928 and was buried in the Brompton Cemetery in London. Her statue was unveiled in Victoria Tower Gardens in 1930, and moved to a more prominent position close to the entrance to the House of Lords in 1955.

Mrs. Anne Cobden-SANDERSON, was born in 1853 in London, the daughter of Richard Cobden. From 1877 she was engaged in social work in the East End. In 1882 she married Thomas James Sanderson, a barrister. They adopted the surname Cobden-Sanderson. They had a son and a daughter. Mrs. Cobden-Sanderson became a good friend of William Morris and later she and her husband established the Doves Press which became an important part of the Arts and Crafts Movement, but she also continued with her social work.

For several years Mrs. Cobden-Sanderson was a member of the NUWSS, but frustrated by its lack of success joined the WSPU. When she was arrested during a demonstration outside the House of Commons and subsequently appeared in court she commented:

> We have talked so much for the Cause now let us suffer for it... I am a law breaker because I want to be a law maker.

In 1907 together with seventy-seven other women who were dissatisfied with the way Christabel and Emmeline Pankhurst were running the WSPU, Mrs. Cobden-Sanderson left to form the WFL. In 1909 she also helped to found the Tax Resistance League. She was a pacifist and refused to support the war effort. Mrs. Cobden-Sanderson died in 1926.

Section 2

Llangollen NUWSS Minute Book and Any Other Business

When Britain declared war on Germany on 4 August 1914, all women's suffrage societies were asked to cease campaigning and support the war effort. Llangollen members were certainly prepared to support the war effort, but decided to continue to meet as Suffragists throughout WW1. The Minute Book of their committee meetings from December 1914 is preserved in The National Library of Wales. Obviously other NUWSS groups continued to meet, as can be seen by accounts of various high-level committees. But the two largest and most influential groups in North Wales: Bangor and Colwyn Bay seem to have disbanded when Mrs. Charlotte Price White and Miss Mildred Spencer, their respective secretaries, devoted themselves entirely to war work for the duration of hostilities.

1914

December

The Llangollen NUWSS committee met at the Women's Club on 3 December, with Mrs. R. Ll. Hughes in the chair. Also present were: Miss Greenland, Mrs. J.E. Hughes, Miss Marwood, Mrs. Morris Roberts and Miss Beatrice Stewart, secretary. (Miss Stewart's hand-writing is clear but when she realised she could not fit a word she had started onto a line, she bent it round and those words are difficult to read – particularly if they are names).

Details were given of the AGM at the Women's Club on 18 November, chaired by Mr. Marwood. Miss Stewart read her own report and the treasurer's (in the absence of Mrs. Wood). Both were adopted and it was agreed that they should be printed and circulated. Cordial thanks were expressed to Mr. Alfred Beardsworth for auditing the accounts. The officers and committee had been re-elected with the exception of Miss Holdsworth and Miss Lloyd, who were replaced by Miss Greenland and Mrs. J.E. Hughes. Mrs. John Aikin was elected vice-president. An informal report on work undertaken since the outbreak of the war was given by Miss Stewart and Mrs. Aiken, who also provided afternoon tea. The collection for charities raised £1-16/-.

The committee decided that as contributions towards the NUWSS bed in the Welsh Hospital at Netley were no longer being accepted, £1-11/- should go to SWH which had been founded by Dr. Elsie Inglis, a fellow Suffragist, and was the NUWSS' special project. The remaining 5/- was to be donated to the fund for Welsh Women Married to Aliens, many of whom obviously experienced extreme financial strictures when their husbands were interned.

The committee then heard a report from the Clubs sub-committee. A Knitting Club was being held every Thursday afternoon. Mrs. Aiken and Madame de Steiger were organising a Reading Club which would meet on alternate Wednesday evenings, the first meeting being the following Wednesday.

Knitting Clubs abounded in WW1 with women, children, and men unable to serve in the military, volunteering to knit balaclavas, cardigans, gloves, mittens, scarves, socks and even long-johns for soldiers. Socks were essential, because only a constant supply of dry socks could prevent soldiers getting Trench Foot in the cold, wet and mud of the trenches. If untreated, this fungal disease could lead to Gangrene and the necessity for amputation. Most women knew how to knit, but those who did not, and children – both boys and girls, soon learned. At first they knitted simple squares which were sewn together to make blankets for refugees, before graduating to socks. It was felt that knitting together in a club was good for both morale and productivity, but knitters were encouraged to continue to pick up their needles whenever they could – at home, whilst attending meetings, on public transport, and some even managed to walk and knit simultaneously. Groups which, for whatever reason could not knit, raised funds to supply wool and needles for the knitters.

As the war progressed, it became obvious that what was needed were sock patterns adapted for standard sizes and once these was produced by the Red Cross, a narrow stripe was knitted into the top of each sock: white for small, blue for medium and red for large, thus ensuring that every soldier received a supply of socks – whatever his foot size.

A letter was read from Mrs. Harley concerning the formation of the Active Service Girl's Cadet Corps. A long and interesting discussion followed and members agreed that work was urgently needed amongst the girls in the town. Mrs. J.E. Hughes offered to start a Hockey Club and this offer was gratefully accepted. Miss Greenland suggested inviting girls into the Women's Club to play games in the evenings, but it was decided that members should be consulted about using the club for this purpose before proceeding. It was agreed that the club committee must be consulted concerning the use of the club; and that Miss Stewart should arrange a meeting with Mrs. Turner and anyone else interested in the welfare of the local girls.

1915
January

The committee met at the Women's Club on 26 January. Miss Stewart stated that as instructed, she had convened a meeting chaired by Mrs. John Aiken earlier in the month, and as a result the following resolution was passed:

> That this meeting of representative women urges the Llangollen War Committee to sanction and assist the establishment of a branch of the League of Honour and further, begs the appointment of a committee for that purpose.

The League of Honour was an organisation for women and girls which appears to have been connected to the Young Women's Christian Association (YWCA). The resolution had been laid before the War Committee and, with the substitution of *approve* for *sanction*, passed by a majority. The position was therefore, that the Central Committee of the League of Honour: representing all religious denominations would form a sub-committee of the War Committee, and it was hoped that each denomination or organisation would run its own branch, with all branches uniting for public meetings.

The committee then discussed the principal resolution on the Agenda for the NUWSS' Annual Council Meeting in London, and was unanimous in disapproving of the line proposed by the executive with regard to the question of war; and further agreed that no delegate or proxy be sent to the council.

Unlike Mrs. Pankhurst, Mrs. Fawcett, the NUWSS Leader, refused to assist with any recruiting strategy for the war effort. She preferred her member's efforts to be directed towards funding the setting up of SWH units abroad.

May

The committee met at Oaklands, home of Miss Stewart, on 29 May. A telegram was read from Mrs. Wood expressing regret at her inability to attend. Miss Stewart informed the members that the League of Honour was being run independently from the Suffrage Society. The Suffrage Society had merged with Llangollen Women's Club and Mrs. Aikin had become registrar and secretary of the Women's Club. The League of Honour, and the joint Suffrage Society and Women's Club would have use of the club premises, now established at the Victoria Stores, Chapel Street. The suffrage library could be found there, and the premises would be open every day except Sunday and every evening except Saturday and Sunday.

Miss Stewart explained that despite the decision taken at the previous committee meeting not to send a delegate or proxy to the NUWSS Annual Council Meeting in London, as a result of later correspondence from the NUWSS

Oaklands, Llangollen – home of Beatrice Stewart, NUWSS secretary and venue for many committee meetings

Council and consultation with Mrs. Wood, they had asked a fellow member, Miss Haggis, whom they knew would be in London at the time of the meeting to attend. She had been unable to do so, and had asked another member, Miss Strachey, who was in London at the time to try to obtain a proxy, but as Miss Stewart had heard nothing from Miss Strachey, she thought it safe to assume than Llangollen had not been represented at the council.

Miss Stewart also told them that one of their members, Nurse Winifred Goodwin, had gone to Serbia with the 2nd Unit SWH. It had therefore been agreed at an informal meeting that members should work to support the hospital to which she was attached. Management of the work would be undertaken by Mrs. Morris Roberts, Miss Ford and Miss Long; and the buying in of materials by Miss Stewart. A resolution confirming this arrangement was passed.

It was agreed that Miss Stewart should be the delegate to the forthcoming Special Council Meeting to be held in Birmingham on 17–18 June and that her fare should be paid from society funds.

The events leading up to the calling of the Special Council Meeting, namely the resignation from the National Executive of the Misses Kathleen Courtney and Catherine Marshall and eleven other members, was discussed. Mrs. Fawcett's letter to local secretaries was read expressing her view that:

> An international meeting of women while the war is still raging is highly undesirable. Women are as subject as men to national prepossessions and susceptibilities ... we should run the risk of the scandal of a peace conference disturbed and perhaps broken up, by violent quarrels

Mrs. Fawcett passionately believed that if leading feminists were, in wartime, to identify themselves as unpatriotic, peace-at-any-pricers, they would sink the cause of women's suffrage in Britain for generations. The Llangollen committee was unanimous in its disapproval of the attitude adopted by the Misses Courtney and Marshall and eleven other members, and cordially approved of the action of the executive in refusing to allow the NUWSS to be represented at the International Congress of Women, which had been held at The Hague the previous month. For some years before WW1 the International Women's Suffrage Alliance had met in alternate years and in 1915 it was due to meet in Berlin. In February that year Aletta Jacobs, the first female doctor in the Netherlands, had held a meeting in Amsterdam attended by four Belgian, four German and five British women, including the Misses Courtney and Marshall, and Miss Chrystal MacMillan (who had spoken at the first NUWSS meeting in Denbigh in 1910). Dr. Jacobs proposed that the Congress should be held at The Hague because the Netherlands was a neutral country. Invitations were sent out requiring those attending to agree to support two preliminary proposals:

> that conflicts should be resolved by peaceful means, and that women should have the right to vote.

Public opinion both in Britain and abroad was very firmly against the Congress meeting during wartime. The British Government issued passports to only twenty-four of the 180

> dangerous women

as Winston Churchill described them, who wished to attend. He subsequently closed the shipping lanes for the duration of the Congress, thus rendering the passports useless!

However, 1,300 women from twelve countries did attend, including three from Britain: Kathleen Courtney and Chrystal MacMillan who were already in the Netherlands, and Mrs. Emmeline Pethick-Lawrence, a prominent Suffragette, who had been lecturing in the United States, and travelled with the American contingent.

No argument about who had caused the current war was permitted and no-one was allowed to speak for more than five minutes. Twenty resolutions were adopted including Hungarian, Rosika Schwimmer's proposal to:

> send delegations to both belligerent and neutral countries to implement the Congress resolutions and to try to bring an end to the war.

Five envoys from both neutral and warring countries were elected to take the twenty resolutions to all European Heads of State, the Pope, and the President of the U.S. The five women, including Chrystal MacMillan made the perilous journey across Europe together, before American, Miss Jane Addams who had chaired the Congress, returned to the U.S. Some of the resolutions were subsequently the basis for the founding of the League of Nations Union at the end of WW1. Miss Addams was awarded the Nobel Peace Prize. The foundations for the Women's International League for Peace and Freedom (WILPF) which is still in existence, were also laid at the Congress.

Back at the Llangollen committee meeting it was agreed that when the committee met at the Women's Club they would donate 1/- towards the upkeep of the premises.

There was an additional note that no letter had yet been received from Nurse Goodwin in Serbia.

June

The committee met at the Women's Club on 11 June. Miss

Stewart gave an account of the WLWC&NW NUWSS Federation Meeting in Chester which she had attended on 31 May. She had learned that the Llangollen Society was entitled to two representatives at the National Council Meeting in Birmingham on 17-18 June which she would be attending. But as the questions to be addressed were so important she had applied to the Birmingham Society for a proxy and Mrs. Elsie Cadbury of Northfield had kindly agreed to act. It was agreed that she should be free to use her discretion in voting both for resolutions, and for membership of the executive. It was noted that she had expressed her intention of voting so far as possible with the federation, in accordance with the advice of Miss Eleanor Rathbone (president, Llangollen NUWSS and chairman, WLWC&NW NUWSS).

July

The committee met at Oaklands on 15 July. Miss Stewart gave details of the half-yearly Council Meeting in Birmingham which she had attended, and added that she had written to Mrs. Cadbury to thank her for acting as proxy for them.

Miss Stewart told members that Miss Fox, Miss Long and Mrs. Morris Roberts were preparing garments to be sent to the 2nd Unit SWH in Serbia; and read a letter dated 3 June from Nurse Goodwin in Valjevo.

December

The committee met at Brookbank, home of Mrs. J.E. Hughes on 17 December. Miss Stewart confirmed that a parcel for the 2nd Unit SWH in Serbia had been dispatched to London on 26 November; and that during November 300 copies of the special *Hospital* number of *The Common Cause* had been sold and the £5 raised donated to SWH.

Miss Stewart then read the Annual Report and Mrs. Wood, the Treasurer's Report.

It was noted that Mr. Beardsworth had not only audited the accounts for 1914 but also kindly offered to audit those for 1915 in time for the AGM, which it was agreed would be held on 28 or 30 December.

Miss Stewart indicated that she wished to resign for the duration of the war, but was persuaded to remain in post. It was decided that Miss Nanson should be approached to act as her assistant. Mrs. Wood undertook to deal with any work in connection with the accounts. Mrs. Turner did not wish to stand for re-election to the committee as she was obliged to be away from home often due to the war, and neither did Madame de Steiger as she would soon be moving away from Llangollen. It was agreed that Mrs. A.O. Williams and Miss Adie Davies should be approached to stand for election to the committee.

It was proposed that Rule 4 should be suspended and the following resolution was passed:

> That all members who are Serving their Country with the Colours be made honorary members of the society and not asked to pay the annual subscription during the duration of the war.

Finally it was agreed that Mrs. Fawcett's New Year's letter concerning *The Common Cause* should be circulated amongst the members.

1916
January
The committee met at Brookbank, on 27 January. Miss Stewart said she was sorry to say that Mrs. Darlington, Miss Adie Davies and Mrs. A.O. Williams had declined to stand for election to the committee. Miss Nanson had consented to do so, but felt that she could not at present undertake the

work of assistant-secretary. However, on a positive note, Mrs. J.M. Jones was willing to stand and would gladly undertake to assist Miss Stewart.

Miss Stewart commented on the AGM which had been held at the Women's Club on 30 December with Mrs. Wood in the chair. Also present at the AGM were: Mrs. Aiken, Mrs. and Miss Burgon, Miss Fox, Miss Greenland, Miss Long, Miss Marwood, Miss Nanson, Mrs. Morris Roberts, and the Misses Stewart. She read the Annual Report and Mrs. Wood gave a summary of the Treasurer's Report 1914-15. It was resolved that both documents should be printed and circulated.

Despite a suggestion by Mrs. John Aikin that there should be a new secretary and treasurer, the chairman, secretary, treasurer and committee were re-elected; with the exception of Mrs. Turner and Madame de Steiger who were replaced by Mrs. J.M. Jones and Miss Nanson. Unfortunately, since this arrangement had been made, Mrs. Jones had gone to work in Liverpool.

Miss Stewart gave a brief statement of receipts and expenditure: she had one shilling and one penny ha'penny in hand. It was agreed that the 5/- still in hand from the collection at the previous AGM should be donated to SWH.

Mrs. Fawcett's letter had been circulated to most of the members.

Miss Stewart was appointed federation delegate for the year.

The principal resolutions on the preliminary agenda of the NUWSS Council to be held in London on 17 February and following days were read and discussed. It was resolved that the delegate to the Federation Committee should be instructed to take up an *attitude antagonistic* to the pro-Labour policy. Miss Greenland mentioned that she might possibly be in London on 17 February, in which case it was agreed that she should represent Llangollen as their delegate.

It was agreed that they should hold a Cake Sale, Tea, and Loan and Housecraft Exhibition on 24 February and Miss Stewart was instructed to obtain the use of the Town Hall (free of charge if possible). Miss Greenland was asked to beg Mrs. Burgon to manage the Tea and Cake-stall. Mrs. Wood volunteered to help. Miss Marwood and Miss Stewart undertook to manage the Loan Exhibition but there was no indication as to where the loans would be sought. Miss Nanson, Mrs. Morris Roberts, Miss Stewart and Mrs. Wood agreed to form a begging committee for tea and cakes and arranged a further meeting of this sub-committee at Lyndonhurst on 1 February.

February

The special meeting of the sub-committee met as arranged. Miss Stewart told members that the council was willing to allow them to use the Town Hall free of charge, except for five-pence for lighting. It was agreed that proceeds should be divided equally between the local Belgian Refugees Fund and SWH; also that Miss Dixon's hat mounts were to be sold by Mrs. Morris Roberts for the Serbian Relief Fund. It was agreed that Lady Trevor should be asked to open the sale and that three-pence should be charged for admission. Further, that Miss Fox and Miss Long should be asked to organise the Housecraft Exhibition, and that the Misses Darlington, Pugh-Jones and Lloyd be asked to provide entertainment. An advertisement was to appear in the *Llangollen Advertiser* that week.

April

On 14 April *The Llangollen Advertiser* published a photograph of Llangollen's League of Honour under the direction of Mrs. Aikin, assisting in agriculture by stone picking on Mr. Trevor Lloyd-Jones' pasture. (Unfortunately the quality is too poor to reproduce).

On the same date the committee met at Brookbank. Miss Stewart reported that Lady Trevor had been unable to open the Cake Sale, Miss Fox and Miss Long had declined to organise the Housecraft Exhibition, and the Misses Darlington, Pugh-Jones and Lloyd were unable to provide the entertainment! Owing to the above, and the fact that the County School's Prize-Giving was on the proposed date, 24 February; it had been decided to postpone the Cake Sale until 23 March. So by the time the committee met, the event had already taken place. Arrangements had been made by the sub-committee chaired by Mrs. Burgon. The Loan Exhibition had been organised by Miss Marwood and Miss Nanson assisted by the Misses Cole, Cross, Jackson and Parry. Three-pence had been charged for admission, and after tea Mrs. J.E. Hughes had recited a Tennyson poem and a gramophone had been lent and operated by Miss M. Parry. Sale proceeds amounted to £12-2-8d which, after all expenses had been paid, left £5 guineas each for the local Belgian Refugees Fund and SWH. The sale of hat mounts had raised 18/8d for the Serbian Relief Fund. A letter of thanks had been received from Miss Cross, secretary of the Belgian Refugees Fund.

Copies of the Annual Report were handed out and Miss Marwood and Miss Nanson offered to distribute copies to society members.

Discussion followed concerning the NUWSS Federation's scheme to support relief for refugee children at Kazau [*sic*]. It was agreed that it was not desirable to arrange a meeting in support, and Miss Stewart's offer to make a collection amongst members was declined. It was agreed that the maternity bag should be offered to the federation for the use of Russian refugees.

June

The committee met at Oaklands on 6 June. Miss Stewart

told members that she had corresponded with Miss McPherson on the subject of the maternity bag. Miss McPherson was of the opinion that it was not desirable to send the bag to Russia and she would very much like it for the Wallasey Maternity Centre, of which she was the secretary. After discussion, it was resolved to keep the bag for the present.

A letter was read from Mrs. Oliver Strachey enclosing resolutions concerning the possible extension of the franchise, passed by the NUWSS Executive. It was resolved that as suggested, copies of the resolutions should be sent to members of the (parliamentary) Cabinet:

> That this committee is of the opinion that, if the proposed Registration Bill brought forward makes no changes in the existing register and is limited to enabling men at the front who are on that register to vote, either by post or otherwise, no women's suffrage amendment is necessary, but if that bill is drafted, or any amendment to it proposes the addition of any fresh person or class of persons to the register without providing for the enfranchisement of women, Suffragists will press for a Women's Suffrage amendment.
>
> Further if the occasion of the Registration Bill provides an opportunity for dealing with the franchise on wide lines, this committee urges the government to include in the bill an agreed clause to remove the political disqualification of women.

The question of the suffrage library, now kept at the Women's Club was discussed, and it was proposed that the librarian should ask Mrs. Aikin to appoint Miss Lily Hughes as assistant-librarian for the League of Honour.

July

The committee met at River View on 25 July. Miss Stewart reported that the resolutions concerning possible registration bills had been sent with a covering letter to the cabinet and replies received were laid before the committee. Miss Stewart also read a letter from Mrs. Oliver Strachey concerning action to be taken with regard to franchise and registration reforms. It was agreed that a delegation to the MP was out of the question, so the following resolution should be signed by all members of the committee and sent to Sir Herbert Roberts:

> That bearing in mind the Prime Minister's declaration on 19 July 1916 that a parliament elected upon a register from which all the men serving their country abroad should be excluded, would be wanting in moral authority, this society considers that, after the splendid national services rendered by women during the present troubles, a parliament elected on a register excluding women would be absolutely destitute of moral force or authority, and therefore presses for the grant of the suffrage to qualified women in every franchise or registration bill that may be passed at the present time.

Miss Stewart was instructed to write to Miss Rathbone stating what had been done and it was agreed that a copy of the resolution should be sent to *The Llangollen Advertiser*. Miss Stewart was also asked to send a message of sympathy to Miss Nanson.

An article in *The Llangollen Advertiser* stated that local Suffragists had sent a petition to Sir Herbert Roberts MP and it was printed verbatim. It was subsequently noted in the newspaper that the franchise question had been adjourned indefinitely.

August

The committee met at River View on 15 August. Miss Stewart reported that the resolution passed at the previous meeting had been duly signed by members of the committee, and forwarded with a covering letter to Sir Herbert Roberts MP. His reply was laid before the committee. Miss Stewart also said that she had written to Miss Rathbone as instructed, enclosing Sir Herbert Roberts' reply for her perusal. Miss Stewart then read a letter from the NUWSS secretary concerning the present position. It was agreed that on receipt of further instructions from the NUWSS, Miss Stewart be empowered to act in consultation with any members of the committee with whom she could conveniently confer.

The minutes of the Federation Meeting in Liverpool on 13 July were laid before the committee and extracts read.

The possibility of forming a study circle for the winter months was discussed and Miss Marwood kindly offered a room for meetings. It was agreed Miss Greenland should ask Mrs. Wheeler if she would lead such a study circle? The question of *International Relations* was suggested as a suitable subject.

It was agreed that Llangollen could not undertake to help with the NUWSS Jumble Sale Scheme.

October

The committee met at River View on 9 October. Miss Stewart brought to their attention a letter from Mrs. Fawcett, asking the societies whether they wished to have a Half-Yearly or Special Council? Miss Stewart informed them that she had, in accordance with the resolution passed at the August meeting, consulted with Mrs. J.E. Hughes and Mrs. Wood, both of whom agreed with her that no council should be held at present, and read her reply to this effect.

Miss Greenland stated that she had approached Mrs.

Wheeler twice on the subject of the study circle, but that she could not undertake to conduct it.

Miss Stewart read a letter from Miss Muriel Price regarding literature concerning *International Relations* and enclosing a list of pamphlets. It was agreed that Mr. Marwood should be asked to take on the study circle, and that if it could be conveniently arranged the circle should meet at the Women's Club.

Miss Stewart read an appeal from SWH. It was agreed that no effort could be organised at the present time, but it would be well to make one early in the spring.

Miss Greenland, Miss Marwood, Mrs. Morris Roberts and Miss Stewart undertook to help Mrs. Wood collect subscriptions.

It was agreed that the AGM should be held in November if possible.

Mrs. Morris Roberts said that she had spoken to Mrs. Aikin about the books in the suffrage library and that Mrs. Aikin would be holding herself responsible for their use by the cadets.

November

The committee met at River View on 8 November. Miss Stewart was pleased to tell members that Mr. Marwood had kindly consented to conduct the Study Circle and that he wished to begin with *The Life of Randolph Churchill*. The first meeting was to be held at the Women's Club on 13 November. Further, Miss Stewart had arranged with Mrs. Aikin that members of the Circle should contribute to the Club box, towards the cost of heating and lighting.

Miss Stewart confirmed that the AGM would be held at the Women's Club on 17 November. Mrs. Aikin had been asked to preside but as she was unable to do so, and Mr. Marwood had agreed to take her place.

Miss Greenland, Miss Marwood, Mrs. Morris Roberts

and Miss Stewart handed over the subscriptions they had collected to Mrs. Wood.

Miss Stewart then read a letter from Miss Atkinson and Miss Eustace of the NUWSS concerning the political situation, and urging upon the societies the importance of sending deputations to MP's. It was agreed that Miss Stewart should write to Miss Rathbone for her advice, suggesting that she should lead a deputation from Colwyn Bay and Llangollen to see Sir Herbert Roberts at Abergele.

Miss Stewart informed the members that the NUWSS was sending out forms to be filled in by women engaged in war-work, and that she was trying to get as many as possible completed by their members.

The committee met at the Women's Club on 17 November. Miss Stewart said that the Study Circle had made a very successful start.

She went on to report that she had written to Miss Rathbone concerning a deputation to Sir Herbert Roberts, and read both Miss Rathbone's reply and a note from Miss Mildred Spencer of Colwyn Bay. It was therefore agreed that Mrs. Aikin should be asked if she was willing to accompany Miss Rathbone to the House of Commons. If this was not possible, then Miss Stewart should write to Miss Rathbone again, suggesting that she should go alone.

Miss Stewart then read the Annual Report and Mrs. Wood read the Treasurer's Report.

The AGM followed, chaired by Mr. Marwood and attended by committee members: Mrs. J.E. Hughes, Mrs. R.Ll. Hughes, Miss Marwood, Miss Nanson, Mrs. Morris Roberts, Miss Stewart and Mrs. Wood; and members: Mrs. Darlington, Mrs. Thomas Davies, Mrs. George Jones and Mrs. Jones (Helenfa).

1917
May
The Llangollen Advertiser carried an item on women's war work. Mrs. Aikin, registrar and secretary of the Women's Club, had reported that although three groups were at work on local farms, many more volunteers were needed. Thirteen armlets had been awarded: three to gardeners, four to women looking after cattle and six to part-time workers. Women had to work for 230 hours to qualify for an armlet. A sub-committee had been formed to do everything possible to increase food production. Miss Wordsworth, County Organiser, had given the newspaper details of the National Service Scheme: women aged twenty or over would receive a month's free training, a minimum wage after training of eighteen shillings per week and free uniform. Women who already had some experience would receive a maintenance grant of fifteen shillings per week whilst undergoing three week's training on a farm. Travelling expenses would be paid, and accommodation in a depot provided during periods of unemployment not exceeding one month. Any woman who worked a minimum of twenty-four hours in one week could buy a pair of boots at the nominal price of 12/- and pay in twelve weekly instalments. Candidates would be interviewed by the Selection Committee of the Women's County Committee which sat at Wrexham every week. Forty-nine Denbighshire women had passed the Selection Committee in the past fortnight and begun their training. Women with agricultural training and practical experience were needed as group leaders: but they would have to be willing to work in any part of the country where they were needed.

Miss Wordsworth was quoted as saying that she did not think some country women fully realised the gravity of the food situation, certainly not as fully as it was understood in the towns. Country women looked to town's women to supply munitions and town's women looked to country women to provide food. (It is worth noting that the second biggest Munitions Factory in Wales was less than twenty miles away, at Queensferry on Deeside. 7,325 members of staff were employed and 70% of those working on the actual munitions were women). Miss Wordworth had concluded that no woman ought to have any leisure while their men were fighting in the trenches, and she was proud that Llangollen had led the way in the Denbighshire in providing groups of female agricultural workers.

The article closed with an offer from Mrs. Aiken to supply Sunflower seeds to anyone who had a sunny spot in their garden to grow them. Sunflowers were, she explained, an excellent food source for poultry.

June

The committee met at River View on 5 June. Miss Stewart apologised for having been unable to attend the Annual Council Meeting in London on 21 February and read a list of those elected to the Executive Committee.

Miss Stewart then told the members that she, together with Mrs. J.E. Hughes and Mrs. Morris Roberts, with some help from non-members i.e. the vicar and Mrs. Allen Lettsome had collected about eighty signatures to the memorial. After she, Miss Stewart, had analysed it and Miss Cole had copied it, Miss Rathbone had sent it to Sir Herbert Roberts, and his reply was read. It was agreed that a copy of the memorial should be sent to the Prime Minister, Mr. Lloyd George. (Unfortunately the memorial was not included in the minutes). Further, Miss Stewart advised that the idea of a joint deputation to MP's from the Welsh NUWSS had been abandoned, but that Miss Rathbone had seen Sir Herbert Roberts at the House of Commons during the spring. Miss Stewart then read a letter from Miss Rathbone concerning this.

Miss Stewart also presented the minutes of the Federation Committee's May meeting in Liverpool, which she had attended.

The draft of The Representation of the People Bill was then laid before the committee and it was agreed that a letter of thanks should be sent to Sir Herbert Roberts for his support.

Finally, copies of the Llangollen Society's Annual Report were handed out.

August

The committee met at River View on 31 August. Miss Stewart explained that she had called a meeting for 12 July but as only three members (including herself) had been able to attend, it was her intention to bring the business before the current meeting. After consultation with the chairman and treasurer she had on 11 June, telegraphed Mrs. Fawcett on the occasion of her seventieth birthday. Miss Stewart read a letter of thanks from Mrs. Fawcett; confirmed that as agreed at the previous meeting she had written to Sir Herbert Roberts thanking him for his support, and read his reply. Further, acting on a letter from the NUWSS she had written to Sir George Cave urging that married women be given the municipal vote. Miss Stewart continued by reading out a message from Mrs. Fawcett published in *The Common Cause* regarding Clause IV of the Representation of the People Bill.

Proposals from the Women's Citizen's Association and Women's Local Government Society were discussed, but it was felt that no additional work could be undertaken at the present time.

There was also discussion concerning a memorial to the late Mrs. Katherine Harley (who had been killed whilst serving with SWH in Serbia), and it was agreed that Llangollen should support the Harley Memorial Loan Fund (in connection with the London School of Medicine). Mrs. Aikin was to be consulted and a collection amongst members of the society undertaken.

Many regrets were expressed that Miss Greenland was leaving the neighbourhood and as a small token of their recognition of her services, particularly as librarian, her fellow committee members presented her with a copy of *With the Red Cross in Serbia*. Miss Marwood kindly volunteered to take charge of the suffrage library.

October

The committee met at River View on 12 October. The treasurer read a letter of thanks for the £1 donation to SWH. Further letters were read from Mrs. Oliver Strachey concerning the Representation of the People Bill; the future of the NUWSS and the extension of the municipal vote to married women. It was agreed that Miss Stewart should approach Mr. Williams with the object of getting a resolution passed in favour of such an amendment to the bill by the Oddfellows Club.* Also that a resolution be sent to the Home Secretary with copies to the Government Whip and Sir Herbert Roberts:

> That this society urges the government to accept on the Report Stage of the Representation of the People Bill one amendment to Clause IV, sub-section 3, extending the municipal vote to the wives of men on the Local Government Register.

Further letters were read regarding the number and particulars of women on the local Food Control Committee and enquiring whether there was a Women's Citizenship Association in the area.

Miss Stewart then informed the members that Miss Lucy Broadbent from Manchester, who had worked for SWH in

London would shortly be visiting Llangollen, and it was agreed that she should be invited to speak at their AGM – the choice of date to be left to her.

Mrs. Morris Roberts volunteered to help the treasurer with collecting subscriptions.

The NUWSS committee met again at River View on 19 October. Miss Stewart reported that the resolution concerning the Municipal Franchise had been sent as agreed. She had spoken to Mr. Williams but had been advised that the Llangollen branch of the Oddfellows did not pass political resolutions.

To accommodate Miss Broadbent the AGM would be held on 1 November. It was agreed that notice cards should be printed for members, Mrs. Aikin should be asked to take the chair and the collection should be given to the Harley Memorial Loan Fund.

*The Oddfellows was essentially a Friendly Society, formed to protect the rights of workers and their families

November

The committee met at The Women's Club on 1 November. The Secretary and Treasurer's Annual Reports were read and both were adopted. It was agreed that 7/- should be paid towards Miss Broadbent's travelling expenses.

1918

March

The committee met at Royal View, the home of Mrs. J.E. Hughes, on 19 March. On the suggestion of Miss Stewart it was agreed to co-opt Miss Holdsworth back onto the committee, and she was accordingly invited to come in and take part in the proceedings. Miss Stewart gave an account of the 1917 AGM which had been held at the Women's Club on 1 November, attended by both members and visitors. A letter from Miss Rathbone was read and she was re-elected president; Mrs. Aikin vice-president; Miss Stewart secretary and Miss L. Cole treasurer. All members of the committee were re-elected with the exception of Miss Greenland who was replaced by Mrs. Wheeler. Miss Broadbent gave a very interesting address and the collection, which amounted to £3-10/- had been forwarded to Mrs. Dymond (Hereford) for the Harley Memorial Loan Fund.

Miss Stewart stated that Clause IV of the Representation of the People Bill had been passed in the House of Lords. On 6 February the Bill had received the Royal Assent and six million women had been added to the electorate. At the same time married women had obtained the municiple franchise.

She explained that she had been unable to attend the WLWC&NW NUWSS Federation Committee and that Miss Cole would have attended the Annual Council Meeting had it been held on 20 February as originally intended, but when it was changed to 12 March she was unable to do so. Miss Rathbone therefore arranged for Miss Eskrigge to act as a proxy representative for Llangollen. Miss Eskrigge had indicated that she would be happy to come to speak to members about what had taken place at council and it was agreed that she should be invited to do so.

There was discussion about the newly formed branch of the National Union of Women Workers and it was agreed that Mrs. Darlington should be asked to represent the Suffrage Society on the local Branch Council.

It was agreed that as the Annual Report had not yet been printed a few words should be inserted stating that the Vote had been won!

At the conclusion of the meeting the chairman made a very appropriate reference to the loss sustained by the society through the death of the late Miss Beatrice Stewart

(Snr.) The secretary, also Miss Beatrice Stewart, (Beatrice Snr's niece) expressed her appreciation for the very beautiful wreath so kindly sent for her aunt's funeral on 9 March. (Hopefully Miss Stewart Snr. knew she had been enfranchised, even though she did not have the opportunity to cast her vote).

May

The committee met at Royal View on 9 May. Miss Stewart reported that Mrs. Darlington was unable to act as representative for the society at the NUWSS Branch Council but Miss Cole had kindly consented to do so. Miss Stewart had seen Miss Eskrigge twice in Liverpool and had tried to arrange for her to come to speak at Llangollen. However, the only date Miss Eskrigge could offer was Friday afternoon 17 May and as this was deemed a most unsuitable time, it was decided to give up the idea of a meeting with her for the time being.

The comment concerning the passing of the Franchise Bill was put before the committee for approval, before being inserted in the Annual Report.

Miss Stewart announced that due to unforeseen circumstances, she was leaving the district almost immediately and must therefore tender her resignation. It was agreed that for the present, letters should be sent to Mrs. John Hughes (chairman) and all secretarial work would be undertaken by Mrs. Hughes and Miss Cole (treasurer).

It was agreed that subject to Mrs. Aikin's consent, back numbers of *The Common Cause* and other Suffrage literature should be housed at the Women's Club. Mrs. Morris Roberts was to take charge of the banner. Miss Nanson kindly undertook to circulate *The Englishwoman*.

At the close of the meeting, on behalf of the society Mrs. Morris Roberts presented Miss Stewart with a very handsome despatch case to commemorate the winning of the vote.

December

The committee met at Royal View on 5 December. The vacancy for a secretary was discussed. It was agreed that the AGM should be held at the Women's Club on 17 December, subject to Mrs. Aikin's approval for the use of the room. Mr. Marwood was to be asked to take the chair and postcards were to be printed inviting members to the meeting.

The committee met at the Women's Club on 17 December and the future of the society was discussed. The AGM followed immediately afterwards chaired by Mr. Marwood. The secretary's and treasurer's reports were adopted and it was resolved to have them printed. Thanks were expressed to Mr. Beardsworth for his auditing of the accounts.

Discussion concerning the future of the society followed and it was unanimously resolved that:

> This society, rejoicing in the success that has attended its efforts, has decided to wind up its affairs and recommends its members to join the National Council of Women;
>
> that the funds in hand be given to the Central Fund of the NUWSS;
>
> that the Library (after certain deductions) be given to Llangollen Free Library;
>
> that the banner given to the society by Miss Beatrice Stewart Snr. be given to the National Council in memory of the Misses Stewart;
>
> that the Maternity Bag be left in the hands of Mrs. Aikin and Mrs. Morris Roberts to be suitably disposed of.

Finally it was agreed that the secretary's and treasurer's reports, together with an account of the AGM should be printed and forwarded to all members.

The fact that Llangollen had a banner suggests that at least some of their members must have taken part in NUWSS demonstrations in London and particularly the 1913 Pilgrimage when women from all over England and Wales walked just a few miles – or all the way to London, to support the cause.

The Report of the AGM noted that:

The able and energetic secretary, Miss Beatrice Stewart, to whom the society, in a great measure, owes its existence, resigned her office on leaving the town. This resignation was accepted with very great regret.

And that the new Llangollen branch of the National Council of Women had:

Gratefully and gracefully accepted the gift of the banner, regarding it as a symbol of the tradition of the work of one of the greatest pioneers in the Women's Movement: the National Union of Women's Suffrage Societies.

They did indeed gratefully and gracefully accept it. Sara Pugh Jones, secretary, wrote:

Thank you for the gift of your beautiful banner. We are a young society and our own history is yet to be made. We are therefore conscious of the privilege in possessing an emblem so historical, an emblem of courage and perseverance in pioneer work for the women of Llangollen. You have handed over to us that which it is generally impossible to give away – a tradition, and we are grateful not only for the banner but for what is symbolises.

What a fitting end for Llangollen NUWSS.

Llangollen NUWSS
Who was Who

The **primary source** of information is the 1911 Census and where ages are given they are the ages in that year. If I have been unable to trace people in 1911 I have looked at the 1901 Census and again, where ages are given they are the ages in that year.
** Biography at the end of this section

Officers and Committee Members:

**Mrs. John G. AIKIN (Bertha)
Miss L.C. COLE (Tyn y wern)
Miss W. GREENLAND
Miss HOLDSWORTH
Mrs. J.E. HUGHES (Margaret A.) (Royal View) secretary
Mrs. R.Ll. HUGHES (Eleanor) (thirty-five) (Osborne House) lived with her husband Robert Llewelyn (thirty-eight) a watchmaker and dealer.
Mrs. J.M. JONES
Miss M. LLOYD
Mr. William and **Miss Flora MARWOOD** (Ely House, Market Street)
William James (fifty-two) (widower) Stationmaster, lived with his daughters: Flora Louisa (twenty-five) teacher and Helena Elizabeth (eighteen).

In April 1916 *The Llangollen Advertiser* published a family notice to the effect that William Edward Marwood of **the Great Western Railway** had married Mabel Alice Tims.

In 1901 **Miss Mabel NANSON** was living with her father Joseph (forty-eight) slate merchant, mother Jane (forty-five), sister Annie (eighteen) and brother Joseph (*no age given*). They employed a cook and housemaid.

**Miss Eleanor RATHBONE

In 1901 **Mrs. Morris ROBERTS (Emma)** (forty-eight) was living with her husband Morris (fifty-five), sons John (twenty-five), George (fourteen), Harry (eight) and daughter Gertrude (sixteen) a milliner. At that time Ellen Taylor (twenty-nine) district nurse, boarded with them.

**Madame Isabel(le) de STEIGER

Miss Beatrice STEWART Jnr. (thirty-seven) (Hafod y Wen, later Oaklands), secretary, lived with her aunts Grace (seventy-five) and Jessie (seventy-three) They employed a companion, housemaid and kitchenmaid. There was another aunt, Beatrice, who does not appear on either this or the 1901 Census.

Mrs. WOOD treasurer

Mr. Alfred BEARDSWORTH (thirty-two) (Bryn Estyn) was a Slate Merchant's Managing Clerk and Llangollen NUWSS auditor, he lived with his wife Isabella (thirty-two).

Supporters:

Mrs. and **Miss BORGON**

Miss Margaret A. CROSS (forty-seven) (Tregweree) lived with her mother Rosetta (seventy-five) and sister Rose (forty-nine). They employed one servant.

Mrs. Emily DARLINGTON (fifty-three), lived with her husband Ralph (fifty-one) publisher, sons Ralph Sydney (twenty-one) and George Blackledge (Darlington) (nineteen); and daughters Emily Kathleen (seventeen) and Enid Gertrude Helen (fifteen). They employed one servant.

Miss Adie DAVIES

Mr. and **Mrs. Thomas DAVIES**

Miss DIXON

Mrs. F. DRINKWATER (Alice) (thirty-four) (The Woodlands) was an American, naturalised on her marriage to Fred (thirty-four) a physician and surgeon. They employed a cook and housemaid.

Miss S.M. FOULKES

Miss FOX

Miss FRANKLIN

Nurse Winifred A. GOODWIN

Miss HAGGIS

Miss HIGGINS

Mrs. Margaret HILL BSc. (2 Bodwen Villas)

Miss Lilian (Lily) HUGHES (thirty-three) assistant suffrage librarian, governess, lived with her mother Amy (sixty-three) and sister Amy (thirty-nine) also a governess. They employed one servant.

Miss Mary Elizabeth JACKSON (thirty-eight) a farmer's daughter, lived with her brothers William (eighteen) farmer and Charles (fourteen); and sister Elizabeth (seventeen) dairy worker.

Also her brother Edward (widower) (forty-two), nephews Edward (ten) and Albert (eight), and niece Mary Charlotte (five) They employed a stockman and general farm worker.

Mrs. E.D. JONES

Mrs. George JONES

Miss H. JONES (Llandrillo)

Mrs. J. JONES (Helenfa)

Miss Sara Pugh-JONES BA (Fron Bache) was born in 1895. She was Llangollen's librarian and an historian. She was also the reporter for, and owner, publisher and distributor of *The Tuesday Review* (1946-67). Early on Monday mornings she travelled either by bicycle and then train, or in her red sports-car (known locally as The Scarlet Runner) to Bala. She spent the day chivvying the type-setter into laying out the content exactly as she wished. She then returned home with the newspapers and spent the evening sorting them into piles for distribution to local newsagents; and attaching wrappers to individual copies to be mailed to ex-locals who had, in her view foolishly, moved away. Finally, she delivered or posted them first thing on Tuesday morning.

When Miss Pugh-Jones retired from the library service in 1967, such was the respect and affection in which she was held that the townspeople presented her with a typewriter; a framed watercolour of Llangollen and a substantial cheque. She died in 1988.

Mrs. LANCASTER

Miss Sally LANGFORD (seventeen), lived with her mother Mary (fifty-one) wool sorter and sister Emily (twelve).

MRS. Allen LETTSOME (Bessie) (thirty-six) (Bryngolen Hill) lived with her husband Allen (thirty-six) photographer and sons Edward Watcyro (Lettsome) (ten) and Charles Brinley (Lettsome) (six), and daughter Gaynor Eleanor (two) (*Mrs. Lettsome was not a committed supporter but helped occasionally*).

Mrs. LEWIS

Miss LONG

Miss Emma Marion OLLEY (forty-five) lived with her brother Henry Robert (fifty-five) headmaster, as his housekeeper, and he employed one servant.

Mrs. E.K. PARRY

Miss M. PARRY

Miss Delia ROWLANDS
Miss F. ROWLANDS
Mrs. Ivor ROWLANDS (Catherine Pryce) (thirty-four)
(45 Castle Street) lived with her husband Ivor (thirty-nine)
baker/confectioner, sons John Morris (eight), Wilfred
Hugh (six) and Thomas Lloyd (four) and her aunt
Catherine Jones (seventy-four). They employed one
servant.
**Miss Beatrice STEWART Snr.
Miss STRACHEY
Miss E.T. THOMAS
Mrs. TURNER
Mrs. Muriel WALTHO (forty-three) (widow) (Fairview)
was a newsagent and tobacconist. She lived with her
daughter Muriel (seventeen) who assisted in the business,
and son Thomas Frederick (twelve). She employed one
servant.
Miss WATSON
Mrs. WHEELER
Mrs. A.O. WILLIAMS
Mrs. WINZAR

Biographies:

Mrs. John G. AIKIN (Bertha) (nèe **Gorst**) Abbey Dingle,
vice-president, librarian.
Mrs. Aikin puzzled me, I could not find her on the 1911
Census, but I could find the Aikin family living at Abbey
Dingle: Louisa Jane (ninety), Charles (sixty-four), and John
G. (fifty-five) (single) retired engineer. They employed a
housekeeper, lady's maid, cook, and housemaid.
    I then checked the marriages and found that in the third
quarter (July-Sept) of 1911, a matter of months after the
census, John G. Aikin had married Bertha Gorst at

A Bertha Aikin bookplate

Oswestry. I then found that the Gorst family was living at Cwm Alis, Llangollen at the time of the census: William Arthur (seventy-two) (widower), Mary Emma (forty-six), **Bertha** (thirty-eight) Artist Etcher, and William Arthur (forty-three). They employed one servant.

In 1928 the Llangollen Welfare House, designed and financed by Mrs. Aikin was opened. It contained an assembly hall with a stage, a room for dentistry and another for sight-testing, a kitchen and a lavatory. The County Medical Services paid a nominal sum to use it for maternity and child welfare services and the Girl Guides met there free of charge. Mrs. Aikin died in 1938.

As I write, in September 2019, Llangollen WI – of which Mrs. Aikin was a founder member, still meets at the Welfare House on the first Thursday in the month, at 2 pm in winter and 7 pm in summer.

Miss Eleanor RATHBONE (chairman WLWC&NW NUWSS), was Llangollen's president. She was born in 1872, daughter of William Rathbone IV, Liberal MP and member of the philanthropic Liverpool shipping and anti-slavery dynasty.

After completing her education at Oxford, Miss

Rathbone immediately returned to Liverpool, where she produced *A Report on the Conditions of Labour at Liverpool Docks*, worked at the Liverpool Central Relief Centre and became the chairman of the Liverpool Society for Women's Suffrage. She was the first woman to be elected to Liverpool City Council. In 1929 Miss Rathbone was elected Independent MP for the Combined Universities and remained in post until her death. She was known for her strong, clear voice and ability to clarify even the most poorly expressed ideas.

She was one of the first to recognise the threat from the Nazi party and in the early 1930's worked to prevent the export of aero-engines to Germany.

Miss Rathbone's most important campaign in parliament was for the Family Allowance Act, which, despite strong opposition, was introduced in 1945. She died in 1946.

Madame Isabel(le) de STEIGER (nèe **Lace**) (Fron/Vron Deg) has been described to me as:

an unlikely Suffragist.

She was born in 1836 in Liverpool. In 1861 she married Rudolph von Steiger von Riggesberg and they settled in Liverpool. By the end of the decade Rudolph had contracted TB and they moved to Egypt in the hope that the climate would prevent further deterioration, but he died in 1872. He left enough money for his widow to live quite comfortably for several decades, so long as she was careful. After Rudoph's death she returned to England, settled in London and took up painting. She exhibited at the Walker Art Gallery, Liverpool, and the Dorothy Restaurants in London, amongst many other places. The Dorothy's (there were two of them) were owned by her friend, Mrs. Cooper-Oakley, a leading feminist. The entrances were painted crimson, rich Indian curtains hung at the windows and there were deep, luxurious couches. The luncheon rooms were furnished with simple tables topped with white, glazed cotton cloths, and vases of flowers. Women customers bought an 8d ticket as they entered, seated themselves at a table and awaited the arrival of their plate of meat, two vegetables and bread. For an extra couple of pence they could enjoy a pudding, and for a further penny, a cup of chocolate, coffee or tea. The Dorothy's became as popular with well-heeled shoppers as they were with the girls who served them – for whom they had originally been established. No men were admitted. But some people were scandalised to glance through the windows and see women openly smoking!

About this time Isabel joined the Order of the Golden Dawn and her subsequent art work and beliefs are extensively covered on-line by Roger Wright and Sally Davis. In 1894 Isabel had a letter published in *Light: a Journal of Psychical, Occult and Mystical Research* in which she wrote that she thought she had seen the same ghostly face in two different photographs, taken several years apart. She meant just that, but many *Light* readers thought she was suggesting fraud – particularly as the second photo was supposed to have been taken during a séance held by a well-known medium, David Dugoid; and its validity had already been questioned by *Practical Photographer*. Eventually Dugoid's photograph was proved to have been faked.

In 1900 Isabel put nearly all her belongings, including her paintings into storage, and they were destroyed by fire, thus depriving her of the one-woman show which she had been promised. During 1914-15 she lived in Llangollen and served on the NUWSS committee. In 1917 her first book:

Superhumanity came out. She died in Liverpool on New Year's Day 1927. The following May her second book: *Memorabilia* was published.

Miss Beatrice STEWART Snr.

On 22 March 1918 *The Llangollen Advertiser* published the following obituary:

> by the passing away of Miss Beatrice Stewart (aged eighty-two), Oaklands, late of Hafod-y-Coed, Llangollen has lost one of its most interesting and striking personalities. Possessed of high mental and moral powers and great force of character, Miss Stewart took a great interest in all social and political questions of the day, especially in those relating to the improvement of the status of women. An ardent Suffragist, she did much to further the cause of women's suffrage and the Llangollen society owes much of the success of the movement in this locality to her unvarying kindness and sympathy. In her quiet, unobtrusive way she did much to help the poor, by whom her loss will be deeply felt. She also took a keen interest in the Cottage Hospital and the Public Library and there are still some residents who remember gratefully that she voluntarily taught needlework in the days of the old Board School. She was a great lover of nature – of flowers and plants in particular, of which she had a wonderful knowledge. Nothing gave her greater pleasure than to be shown a rare or little-known plant.
>
> Miss Stewart bore an extraordinary resemblance to her late majesty, Queen Victoria and many will remember the tableau vivant performed in the year of the Jubilee 1897, when she was persuaded to impersonate the late Queen, which she did with most marked success ...

the final tableau was an astonishingly faithful likeness of Her Majesty, so faithful indeed that there was a touch of heartfelt devotion and loyalty in the singing of *God Save the Queen* by the audience, as the entertainment drew to a close.

Miss Stewart was laid to rest in the Churchyard at Llantysilio and many friends assembled to do honour to her memory. Some beautiful wreaths were sent, conspicuous among them being one from Llangollen Women's Suffrage Society, of which she had been a member since its foundation.

Proxy's:

Mrs. Elizabeth (Elsie) CADBURY (nèe **Taylor**) acted as proxy for Llangollen when no-one could attend and therefore vote at a National Council Meeting in Birmingham in 1915.

Elsie Cadbury

She was born in 1858, one of ten children. Her parents, John and Mary, were Quakers, temperance crusaders and adult education supporters, living in London. Elsie and her sister Margaret were tutored privately in Germany and Elsie completed her education in London. She then taught the younger children in her family, as well as a class of forty boys at a Quaker Sunday School in a poor district in south London. She went on to form a boy's club for them. On a visit to her aunt and uncle in Birmingham she met George Cadbury, and due to their mutual interests in adult education and temperance, they became friends and worked as colleagues for ten years.

After the death of his wife in 1887, George confided in Elsie his sense of loss and his sorrow for his five motherless children. They became close and married in 1888. They had six more children together and the whole family moved to The Manor at Northfield. She was a devoted wife and mother and although they employed governesses, never a day passed when Elsie did not spend time with their children.

A large hall – The Barn was built at The Manor, and Elsie gave an annual party for around 700 of the poorest children from Birmingham.

Elsie was influential in the development of the Bournville Estate for Cadbury workers, situated on the edge of the countryside, away from the smoke and grime of the city. In 1900, with her complete support, George gave away most of his wealth and formed the Bournville Trust to run the idyllic village of 370 cottages. There was a swimming pool with heated changing rooms, and sports fields. The Beeches – which provided holiday accommodation, again, for poor children from the city was also built. In 1906 Cadbury's was one of the first firms in the country to offer a pension scheme.

With the outbreak of war, George and Elsie encouraged their male workers to follow their consciences – even though, as Quakers, they were pacifists. Men were assured that their jobs would be held open for their return. Cadbury's provided financial assistance to any workers suffering hardship due to limited chocolate production resulting in reduced working hours; to the families of employees who had enlisted; and to widows and dependents of men killed in action. During WW1, Cadbury's sent 20,000 parcels of chocolate, books and warm clothing – knitted by Cadbury's employees, to troops at the front and in hospitals. They set up convalescent homes to allow the injured time to recover, and in cases where men were unfit to return to their original posts, offered re-training.

After the war Elsie, together with other Quakers, brought fifteen orphaned Austrian children to live at Bourneville and organised Cocoa Rooms in Vienna where other children in the same plight could be fed. In 1918 she was honoured for her war work with the OBE, and by the Belgian Government, and the Red Cross in Greece, Serbia and Yugoslavia. In 1934 she was made a DBE. She also received an Honorary MA from Birmingham University for Services to Education and the City of Birmingham. She died in 1951 and reports of her death tell how much she was loved in the city. She was buried in the Friends Meeting House (Quaker) Burial Ground at Bournville.

Edith Eskrigge,
N. Wales NUWSS Organiser

Miss Edith ESKRIGGE acted as proxy for

Llangollen when no-one could attend and therefore vote at the NUWSS Annual Council Meeting in March 1918. She was born in 1872 in Liscard on the Wirral. She was the WLWC&NW NUWSS Organiser. During WW1 she worked for the Liverpool War Pensions Committee and the Sailor's Families Association. With Eleanor Rathbone she established Invalid Children's Aid which became the Child Welfare Association, in the city. Miss Eskrigge was also active in the Child Adoption Society. At the end of the war she became secretary of the Liverpool Women's Citizenship Organisation. She died in 1948.

Section 3

The Welsh Hospital, Netley, Southampton

The Royal Victoria Military Hospital, Netley, Southampton had opened somewhat belatedly in 1856 to provide treatment for men injured in the Crimean War. The actual hospital was a quarter of a mile long with its own reservoir, gasworks, bakery, stables, school and even prison on site. During WW1 the dreaded D block was added: England's first purpose-built military asylum, where men suffering from extreme psychosis as a result of shellshock were treated; or in some cases, simply locked in padded cells. There was also a grand officer's mess complete with a ballroom, and a swimming pool with water pumped from the sea. There was a shop selling such items as clay pipes and postcards of the hospital.

But even the vast edifice of the Royal Victoria was unable to cope with the number of wounded soldiers returning from WW1; and a new hospital of huts quickly built from kits (politically incorrectly designed by a German company) was constructed in the grounds behind the main hospital. This was The Welsh Hospital, built, equipped and funded entirely by the people of Wales, but not exclusively for the use of Welsh casualties. It was well supported by members of the NUWSS. Often three trains per day brought the wounded to Netley's own station. Many more arrived by sea at Southampton docks and were transferred into waiting ambulances. The Welsh poet, Wilfred Owen was briefly treated here in 1917.

The Welsh Hospital, Netley

Philip Hoare, the author of *Spike Island – The Memory of a Military Hospital* and a *Guardian* article in 2014, explained that when Conan Doyle published his first Sherlock Holmes mystery, *A Study in Scarlet*, and mentioned that Dr. Watson had trained as an army doctor at Netley, none of his readers would have been in any doubt about where and what Netley was. Today, I doubt if many people are aware that it ever existed.

Philip Hoare (who was brought up in Southampton, close to the hospital) continued that the Royal Victoria Military Hospital was, according to a 1900 report:

England's largest palace of pain ...

Netley was the closest British civilians came to the reality of what was happening in Europe. The infrastructure needed to supply and staff Netley meant that the local population knew better than most the true horror of the war – a story carefully concealed from the rest of the country by a government wary of its effect on morale ...

At Netley young nurses, often in their teens and with no previous medical experience, had to deal with men without limbs or faces. Men who'd lost their minds to war.

On 9 October 1914 it was reported in *The North Wales Chronicle* that the people of Wales had raised £21,700 and there were promises of a further £5,000. £25,000 was considered more than adequate to meet the costs incurred in building the huts, equipping the 100 bedded hospital and running it for the first six months, as well as allowing for a contingency fund. There was not the slightest doubt that, should the war be prolonged and further funds needed, the Welsh people would raise whatever sums were required.

Wounded German Prisoners of War were treated at Netley to the understandable disgust of local people. At one point shipyard workers downed tools and marched to the gates to demand that the British soldiers should be housed in the main building, and the POWs relegated to the huts. What the ship-builders did not know was that the huts housed far more modern life-saving equipment, and the brick building was regarded as offering greater security for holding prisoners. It was claimed that the German prisoner's convalescent uniforms had red dots on the back, so that they could easily be identified and shot if they attempted to escape.

On a lighter note, a very youthful Noel Coward performed here with a touring theatre group. There were sports days, jazz sessions and even Gilbert and Sullivan operas performed by staff, and male patients in drag.

In November 1914 it was mentioned in *The Western Mail* that a recreation room had been added to the facilities, and an appeal was made for gifts of cigarettes, pipes and tobacco, fruit, games, and a gramophone and records, for the

The Mikado performed by Welsh Hospital staff, and male patients in drag

wounded soldiers. To us it seems unbelievable that Fag Days were held specifically to raise money for *smokes*!

Another scheme which benefited Netley was the National Egg Collection for the Wounded. The Editor of *Poultry World*, Frederick Carl, had suggested the scheme. The magazine claimed that:

Every British hen should be on active service.

Over a million newly laid eggs were distributed every week not only to military hospitals in Britain, but wherever wounded soldiers were being nursed in France and Belgium. Some eggs were sent directly to local hospitals, but this was discouraged by *Poultry World*. There were over 2,000 depots run by local groups. Special boxes and labels were provided by the magazine and eggs were transported free of charge by rail. A central collection point was established in

London for eggs destined for the south of England and abroad. It was at a warehouse provided, again free of charge, by Harrods. The collection scheme was very popular with children and donors were encouraged to write their name, address and a message on the eggs (Eggograms), and often the recipients wrote to thank the donors.

Queen Mary's Needlework Guild members preparing
Sphagnum Moss dressings

North Wales in particular, was crucial in supplying innovative dressings during WW1. School children in Betws-y-coed regularly picked sack-fulls of Sphagnum Moss which were sent down the valley by train, to the ladies at the The Deganwy branch of Queen Mary's Needlework Guild. (QM's Needlework Guild). They selected all the clean moss and weighed it into two ounce packages which were described as being

like gold

by the nurses who used the dressings – so effective were they in aiding the healing of wounds.

Christmas was always celebrated at the Welsh Hospital with the staff trying hard to make it as enjoyable as possible for their patients, some of whom were thousands of miles away from home. But perhaps that first Christmas was the most memorable due to the foresight of HRH Princess Mary. She realised that nearly every family in Britain would have someone missing from their Christmas celebrations, and approached the government with her idea – which was to create Princess Mary's Sailor's and Soldier's Fund to ensure that:

> Every sailor afloat and every soldier at the front will receive a Christmas present from 'home' on 25 December

financed not by the Royal family, but by the general public!

A government committee was set up which decided that the gift should be an embossed brass tin containing a number of small items, and that 145,000 sailors and 350,000 soldiers would receive one. The estimated cost was put at £55,000. The initial response to the appeal resulted in £170,000 pouring in and the government decided that it could afford to distribute the tins to all 2,620,019 service personnel whether they were afloat or at the front – or not. The list included wounded soldiers, prisoners of war (whose boxes were kept for them), nurses tending the wounded, and parents and widows of those who had already been killed in action.

In November a letter from Princess Mary regarding her fund was published in every British and Colonial newspaper, and again the response was so overwhelming that the government committee ordered hinged brass tins 5" x 3½" x 1" deep, with Princess Mary's silhouette and monogram enclosed in a laurel wreath embossed in the centre; the names of allied countries around the edge, and

Christmas 1914 beneath the silhouette and monogram. Smokers received one ounce of tobacco, a pipe, twenty cigarettes and a tinder-lighter; non-smokers a packet of acid tablets (sweets – not for indigestion!), a khaki case of writing paper and a bullet-shaped lead pencil; and nurses, chocolates. Everyone received a photograph of Princess Mary and a Christmas card printed with the message:

> Best wishes for a Happy Christmas and Victorious New Year from Princess Mary and friends at home.

Brass, a key component in military equipment, was in short supply and so some personnel did not receive their gifts until the new year (their tins were embossed 1915 and they received a New Year card), but patients at the Welsh Hospital received theirs on Christmas Day.

There were carols on Christmas Eve, brightly coloured decorations, medical officers carved turkeys on the wards, Lady Violet Mond provided plum puddings, and concert parties visited in the evening. These traditions continued throughout the war. From 1915 Princess Mary's tin was replaced by cigarette cases and match tins engraved:

> The Welsh Hospital, Netley

and the appropriate year, for patients; and cigarettes and chocolate for male and female staff respectively, the gifts of Sir William James Thomas.

At the end of January **1915** it was stated in *The Western Mail* that an additional 100 beds were to be added to the 100 already existing at the Welsh Hospital; that work was starting immediately, and equipment was already being purchased and staff engaged. A twelve bedded hut was also to be provided for officer ranks.

The hospital nursed many Hindus and Sikhs and when a Hindu soldier, Jemadar Harak Bahadur Thapa sadly died from his wounds, the hospital went to great lengths to respect Hindu customs. At home in India, the soldier's body would have been burned on a funeral pyre beside a sacred river. *The Nottingham Evening Post 26 February* carried a description of the ceremony at Netley. A ghat (concrete platform) had been built to accommodate the funeral pyre, beside which a trench was dug. Hundreds of gallons of water were brought up from Southampton and whilst the cremation was being conducted by several high caste Indians, the water was released to give the impression of a flowing stream. Finally, the soldier's ashes were returned to India to be scattered on the River Ganges for his journey to the next life.

In July the *Cambrian News* contained a report on a Royal Visit by HRH Princess Henry of Battenberg (Princess Beatrice of the UK). The hospital's star patient at the time, standing upright and apparently in the best of health, described to the Princess long months in bed and several operations due to Frostbite, followed by a number of weeks in a wheelchair. But due to the kindness of Mr. J. Stubbs of Cardiff, an artificial limb maker, who had presented him with two beautifully made legs, he was now able to walk again.

The Princess was clearly impressed with the clean, bright, blue and white colour scheme and airy spaciousness of the wards. The kitchens (where dinner was being prepared), the nurse's quarters, the pathology laboratory and X-ray departments were inspected. There was also an operating theatre, but this did not feature in the tour. Before she left, Princess Beatrice expressed her gratitude to the people of Wales for providing such an excellent hospital.

Another report contained details of rotary machines for

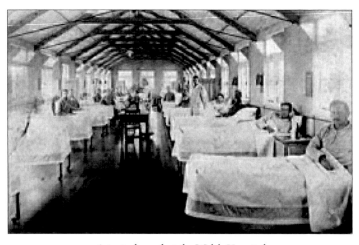

A typical ward at the Welsh Hospital

loosening stiff joints; hot whirlpool baths of varying sizes where patients could soothe injured limbs and nurses could treat chilblained fingers in the winter. There was also a magnetic machine used for removing shrapnel fragments from soldier's eyes. One hut was completely open on one side for nursing TB patients, who were well wrapped up in blankets, and constantly plied with hot water bottles – HM Queen Victoria having personally provided fifty of these. The ward could be chilly for staff, especially at night, although they did have a coal fire in the winter.

Another hut provided occupational therapy, where convalescents could pursue a variety of crafts including basketry, carpentry – especially toy making, drawn thread work, and both silk and wool embroidery. A silk altar cloth for St. Paul's Cathedral embroidered by the patients, was used for the first time on 6 July 1919 at the National Service of Thanksgiving for Peace, in the presence of the King and Queen and many of the 138 soldiers from the UK, Australia, Canada and South Africa who had stitched it. St. Paul's altar was destroyed by bombing in WW2 but the cloth survived.

*Basket weaving at
the Welsh Hospital*

Toy making

*Silk and wool
embroidery*

It has been restored and was used at a service in 2014 to commemorate Britain joining WW1. As a result of an international appeal, the service was attended by many descendants of the embroiderers.

The main thoroughfare between the huts was fondly known as Piccadilly Circus, and the huts which comprised the nurse's homes became Petticoat Lane. The nurse's cubicles were described as being:

white and having electric light, a bed and a simple suite of furniture.

In March an account of St. David's Day celebrations at the Welsh Hospital was carried in *The Cambria Daily Leader* describing how staff wore leeks and the wards were decorated with Daffodils. Mrs. Lloyd George had sent each patient a gift of cigarettes or tobacco, and at tea-time they each had a ration of cake. Many patients joined in singing Welsh songs during the day.

In September *The Brecon and Radnor Express* carried an account of Mrs. Lloyd George and her daughter, Megan's visit to the hospital. They spoke with some of the patients, particularly those occupying the endowed beds. An Irishman was occupying the Women's Suffrage Bed and he declared it very comfortable, and expressed his sympathy with The Cause – although he did not approve of Suffragettes smashing shop windows! There was a Welsh Dog's Bed (not literally), the money to fund it having been collected by dogs in costume (and their owners) throughout Wales. An album containing photographs of the dogs was particularly appreciated by Megan. Horses were also represented, the money to fund their bed having been raised at a military pageant at Cardiff Arms Park.

Also in September, it was reported in *The Flintshire Observer* that there had been great sympathy at the Welsh Hospital for a young man who had arrived suffering from loss of memory and speech, and having no papers. After a few days he was offered a pen, ink and paper and was able to write: *Grange, Rhyl.* A message was sent to the address and the patient, who was only twenty-one years of age, was identified by his aunt (who was living in Rhyl with his two sisters) as Lieutenant David Watkin Hamlen-Williams, son of the late Dr. Theophilus Richard Hamlen-Williams.

The Welsh Hospital, Netley
Patients and Patrons
Who was Who

Patients:

Jemadar Harak Bahadur Thapa was a soldier with the 2nd Battalion Garhwal Rifles, one of the first to leave India to fight for Britain. He died at Netley in February 1916.

Lieut. David Watkin Hamlen-WILLIAMS was born in 1896, the son of Dr. Theophilus Hamlen-Williams. David was educated at Charterhouse and in WW1 served in the 1st Battalion, Herefordshire Regiment (Territorials). He arrived at the Welsh Hospital in September 1916. In October the *Cambrian News* carried a report that Lieut. Hamlen-Williams had lost his memory and

Lieut. David Watkin Hamlen-Williams

speech through shock, and had been invalided from the Gallipoli Peninsula during recent fighting. He received the Silver Wound Badge. He later served with the 4th Battalion, Monmouthshire Regiment.

In 1939, now with the rank of Captain, David Hamlen-Williams, was appointed Lieutenant of the Territorial's National Defence Companies and in 1961 became High Sheriff of Monmouthshire. He died in 1990 at the age of ninety-six at the family farm, St. Mary's, Kingsland.

His family history is well worth recording. His grandfather was Mr. Hamlen of Weston Super Mare. Both he and his wife died and their son, Theophilus Richard, then aged eight, was adopted by his uncle the Rev. David Watkin Williams, Squire of Fairfield, Kingsland. Theophilus qualified as a doctor: MRCS LRCP and worked for a short time at the Middlesex Hospital in London. But he preferred country life, and after his uncle's death he inherited the

Dr. Theophilus Richard Hamlen-Williams

Fairfield estate and title of Squire. In due course he married his uncle's widow, Mary Catherine Williams (nèe Renwick of Llangollen) and added Williams to Hamlen by Royal Assent. The wedding took place in 1893 at The Church of Heavenly Rest in New York.

So popular were Theophilus and Mary in Kingsland that £150 was collected for a wedding present within a few days, and this could easily have been trebled had the fund been left open for longer. The gifts were a large, inscribed, silver bowl on an ebony pedestal and two massive five-branched silver candlesticks. When the Hamlen-Williams' heard about the forthcoming presentation they invited all the subscribers (about 300 – including many of their tenant farmers) to lunch at Fairfield. It was a beautiful, sunny day and the flowerbeds were in full bloom. The men were served in a marquee and the women at a long table on the greensward beneath the trees. It was a sumptuous dinner with all tastes catered for, followed by outdoor games for the young people, and speeches – Mary being proclaimed:

> a shining light, unfailingly kind to the poor, sick and elderly.

The day was rounded off with entertainment by a local choir.

David was born in 1894 and Gwynor Mostyn and Violet Gwenllian (presumably twins) in 1895. Although Mary appeared to be well after the birth of her daughters she suddenly, rapidly deteriorated and died, even before her distraught mother had arrived from Llangollen. She was thirty-six. Mary had asked for her coffin to be covered with a white cloth and strewn with flowers. Her last words to Theophilus were:

> I am weary, let me go home.

Subsequently, in 1898, Theophilus married Mary's youngest sister, Emily Sarah Renwick. They lived at Fairfield and later at The Shrublands, Leominster. Emily took over where Mary had left off and was tremendously kind to needy people. She also took a great interest in farming and was president of many Agricultural Shows. Theophilus was noted for his generosity. He killed a bullock every Christmas to ensure that no-one in the district went without a beef Christmas Dinner, and he annually paid for in the region of three hundred beef, parsnips and potatoes Christmas Dinners, followed by plum pudding, for those in the Workhouse. He also ensured that everyone was able to celebrate events of national importance e.g. HM Queen Victoria's Diamond Jubilee in 1897 and HM King Edward VII's Coronation in 1902.

But surely his most magnificent act of charity was in 1898 when the Welsh miners were on strike – protesting about their wages being linked to the current price of coal. One Saturday morning Theophilus sent his male employees out to visit every workman's home to ascertain who was on strike and needed support. He had killed a fat bullock, many sheep and several porkers, and purchased twelve sacks of the fine potatoes. The neediest families were given tickets and that afternoon 1,500 men, women and boys collected sufficient meat and potatoes to provide Sunday dinners for their families. Since the strike had begun, Theophilus had been providing breakfasts every day in his own kitchen for the wives of strikers to collect, and take home for their families. This continued for the duration of the six months strike. Further, he employed about forty of the strikers in his fields at the rate of 3/- per day and contributed £100 to the strike fund. A local minister observed:

Lord, if this is Toryism, make us all Tories!

On 18 February 1905 – exactly 10 years to the day after Mary had died, Theophilus died of

An affection [*sic*] of the heart.

His coffin was borne by his estate workers and his funeral was described as:

> A demonstration of sympathy for the esteem in which he was held.

Emily continued to bring up her sister's children and kept up her husband's traditions of philanthropy – particularly the gift of a bullock every year to provide beef Christmas Dinners for the needy.

Patrons:

Lady Violet Florence Mabel MOND, Baroness MELCHETT, DBE, (nèe **Goetze**).
In 1894 Violet married Alfred Mond, an industrialist, politician and philanthropist who was created a Baronet in 1910 and Baron Melchett in 1928. They had four children.

Sir Alfred Mond financed the Queen Alexandra's Hospital for Officers in London, which received 900 of the worst cases from WW1, and pioneered surgery to restore the use of their damaged limbs. Afterwards the men convalesced at the Mond's country house, Melchett Court. Lady Mond also loaned their London House to Belgian refugees and it was for these acts of kindness and generosity that she was awarded the DBE in 1920.

She chaired the management committee of the Violet Mond Centre in London, which combined an infant welfare centre, day nursery and home for mothers.

Mr. J. J. STUBBS advertised:

> A boon to the lame ... The motions and actions are as near like a natural foot as possible, no springs, bolts, etc.,

to get out of order. The yielding and elastic qualities of rubber supply requisite motion; avoid all jars to the stump when walking; absolutely noiseless.

Sir William James THOMAS, was born in 1867 in Caerphilly, the son of Thomas and Jane. He was orphaned at an early age and brought up by his paternal grandmother. On leaving school William was employed by his grandfather in the coal industry and inherited the family business. He showed great acumen in running the business as well as real concern for the welfare of his employees. He was a generous philanthropist supporting many medical charities, including giving a donation of £100,000 to the Welsh National School of Medicine.

He was knighted in 1914 and created a Baronet in 1919. He was a councillor, a magistrate, became a freeman of Cardiff in 1915 and High Sheriff of Glamorgan in 1936. He received an honorary degree from Cardiff University, and was elected vice-chancellor in 1931.

He married Maud Mary Cooper, Deputy-Matron of Cardiff Royal Infirmary in 1917. He was a lifelong member of Saron Welsh Congregational Church, Ynyshir, Rhondda Valley. He died in 1945.

Section 4

Scottish Women's Hospitals (for service abroad)

Before WW1 Dr. Elsie Inglis, who founded SWH, had been secretary of the Scottish Federation of Women's Suffrage Societies. SWH was set up with two specific aims: firstly to help the war effort by providing medical assistance, and secondly to promote the cause of women's rights – and by their involvement in the war, to win those rights. No wonder they were keenly supported by the NUWSS. The cause was particularly close to the hearts of the Llangollen Suffragists because one of their members, Nurse Winifred Goodwin, was serving in Serbia.

Fund raising originally commenced with the intention of establishing a hospital in Edinburgh to treat war-wounded. However, when Dr. Inglis met with the War Office to offer the hospital to the British Army, she was left in no doubt that the War

Dr. Elsie Inglis, founder, SWH

Office did not consider it needed her help, being instructed to:

Go home and sit still woman.

So the proposed Edinburgh hospital was abandoned in favour of setting up field hospitals close to the fighting. These were offered to the allies and the first to accept were the French and Belgians, closely followed by the Serbs. They were all grateful for any help – due to the dire conditions their soldiers were suffering. By November **1914** a hospital was opened, equipped and staffed at Calais to treat the Belgian army, followed in December by Royaumont which treated French soldiers under the direction of the French Red Cross. Two further hospitals and three canteens for the use of the French and Belgians were established.

SWH provided doctors, surgeons, nurses, orderlies, ambulance drivers, cooks and administration staff – all female, to staff front line hospitals, field hospitals, dressing stations and canteens. They served in France, Serbia, Corsica, Salonica, Greece, Romania and Macedonia.

In December 1914 it was found that the Serbian Army had only 300 doctors to treat more than 500,000 men. In addition to casualties, they were trying to deal with a Typhus epidemic which was decimating both the military and the civilian population. Soon the Serbian Army had four SWH units at its disposal, but still hundreds of thousands perished.

By the winter of **1915** the Serbs could hold out no longer and were forced to retreat into Albania, leaving SWH staff with a terrible to choice – to stay, or to go with the retreating army. Some stayed and some went, Dr. Inglis was amongst those taken prisoner and eventually repatriated to Britain.

Those who made it to the safety of the Adriatic coast set up a SWH Convalescent Home in Corsica to help displaced Serbian women and children, as well as continuing to do what they could for the armed forces.

One of the French hospitals, which had been designed as a mobile unit equipped with tents and vehicles was dispatched to assist the Serbs. The Girton and Newnham Unit funded by UC Cambridge, was attached to a division of the French Army and sent to Salonica. Much of the work undertaken there was to try to prevent the spread of Malaria, which was a huge killer in the area. The unit was later supplemented by an American Unit and a SWH Transport Unit which allowed the nurses to get to the injured quickly in ambulances, rather than waiting for the casualties to be brought to them. All these units then moved to Ostrovo to support the Serbian Army's push back into its own country.

As soon as Dr. Inglis was repatriated in February **1916** she set about equipping and staffing a hospital to serve in Russia and Romania; together with a Transport Unit

A SWH Transport Unit on the road

providing care mainly to the Serbian Division of the Russian Army, which by this time had no medical facilities whatsoever.

In **1917** SWH staff members were once again forced to endure terrible hardship when they had to take part in a chaotic retreat, as a result of the Romanian Army being routed.

With the onset of the Russian Revolution it soon became clear that the Russian Army was unlikely to re-form and SWH felt it had no option but to withdraw. The women were forced to sail from Archangel through submarine infested waters, back to Britain. Tragically, Dr. Inglis, who had been very ill for some time, died the day after reaching home.

By this time the War Office had done a u-turn. Realising that they did indeed need as many female doctors and nurses as they could recruit, they actively forbade women to join such organisations as SWH. But many women got around this by enlisting as orderlies and drivers – categories not covered by the restrictions. And a new hospital, the Elsie Inglis Unit was sent out to join the Girton, Newnham and American Units, which were still providing medical services to the Serbian Army in Macedonia.

Towards the end of the war SWH actually moved into Serbia – caring for soldiers, civilians and prisoners of war; as well as helping refugees in Corsica and patients at a TB hospital they had established in France. In **1919** the Serbian Hospital was handed over to the Serbian people, but some women chose to stay on to provide still much needed medical care.

Over 1,500 women from many different backgrounds and countries served with SWH and it is estimated that hundreds of thousands of lives were saved by these extraordinary and courageous women.

Two Welsh doctors are known to have served with SWH: Dr. Mary Eppynt Phillips from South Wales and Dr. Helena Jones from North Wales.

Scottish Women's Hospitals
Who was Who

Dr. Elsie INGLIS, was born in 1864 in India. Her father, John, was employed by the East India Company. They arrived in Edinburgh in 1878 and after completing her education and attending finishing school in Paris, Elsie began her training at the Edinburgh School of Medicine for Women. Later she transferred to the rival Medical College for Women. She then studied at the Glasgow Royal Infirmary for eighteen months, before qualifying as a Licentiate at the Colleges of Physicians and Surgeons in Edinburgh and Glasgow.

Next Dr. Inglis worked in London, before returning to Edinburgh in 1894 and setting up as a GP. She later opened a small hospital for women and children, as well as lecturing in gynaecology. She was nearly fifty when war was declared, but her age did not deter her from wholeheartedly volunteering for the war effort, and support for SWH came not only from Suffragists but from women in all walks of life.

Dr. Inglis was the first woman to be decorated with Serbia's Order of the White Eagle – for conspicuous bravery in the field. After her death her body lay in state in St. Giles Cathedral before her burial at Dean Cemetery, Edinburgh.

Money remaining after the end of WW1 was used to build the Elsie Inglis Memorial Maternity Hospital in Edinburgh, which opened in 1925.

Even today she is remembered as the Scottish Mother of Serbia, and in 2015 she and five other women from SWH appeared on commemorative Serbian postage stamps.

Dr. Mary Elizabeth (Eppynt) PHILLIPS was born in 1874 in Merthyr Cynog. In 1898 she was the first woman to qualify as a doctor at a Welsh University: South Wales and Monmouthshire (now UC Cardiff). She completed her training at the Royal Free Hospital in London. In 1904 she was elected to the British Gynaecological Society and in 1905 opened a private clinic in Leeds. Her pre and post-natal care was well ahead of its time. In 1909 she became temporary Medical Inspector for Leeds Schools.

She was an active Suffragist and added Eppynt (the area where she was brought up in mid-Wales) to her name to try to prevent confusion with Mary Phillips – the militant Suffragette. Towards the end of 1914 Dr. Phillips was invited by Dr. Inglis to join SWH and served in France and Serbia before being invalided home with a fever. As soon as she recovered she embarked on a lecture tour to raise funds for SWH. She was known to be an accomplished speaker in both Welsh and English. Later she joined SWH in Corsica. She was awarded the medal of the Order of St. Sava IV by King Peter of Serbia and was also

Dr. Mary Eppynt Phillips

decorated by Britain and France.

From 1920-1929 she was Assistant Medical Officer of Health and Assistant Schools Medical Officer in Merthyr Tydfil. During her retirement she travelled extensively and continued to lecture in order to raise funds for Serbian refugees and deprived children in South Wales. She died in 1956 and was buried in Merthyr Cynog Churchyard.

Dr Helena JONES was born in Conway in 1870, orphaned at the age of six, and brought up in Caernarfon. She too trained at the Royal Free and qualified in 1901. She became the first School's Medical Officer in Yorkshire and later took up the same post in Birmingham.

She was a passionate Suffragette and well respected within the WSPU. An able speaker in her own right, she chaired meetings in North Wales addressed by Mrs. Pankhurst, and Mary Gawthorpe – whom she regarded as a friend.

In 1914 she joined SWH in Corsica. In 1916 she returned to Wales and was appointed Assistant Medical Officer for the Rhondda Valley and remained in this post until her retirement in 1935.

At the outbreak of WW2 she voluntarily came out of retirement and worked as Medical Lecturer to the Red Cross and St. John Ambulance in Cwmparc and Treorchy. During the blitz she was frequently the first doctor on the scene and despite being seventy years of age, worked with willingness, energy and toughness, completely unconcerned about any danger to herself. She died in 1946 and her obituary said:

Her memory will be cherished for all time in the Rhondda Valley.

Section 5

Llanfairpwll Women's Institute

After I had given a talk to a local history society about the North Wales Suffragists, a gentleman commented:

> What did these women (Suffragists and Suffragettes) do after they got the vote?
> They don't strike me as being the sort of women who would be content to sit around drinking tea and eating cake ...

but in a way they were. One of the things many of them supported was the Women's Institute, and it was one of the primary requirements of the WI that members should be able to socialise whilst enjoying tea and homemade cake!

Both the first chairman, Lady Denman, and vice chairman, Miss Grace Haddow, of the Women's Institute in Britain had supported the Suffragists campaign for the vote. Indeed in 1918 Miss Haddow wrote in the *Journal of the Board of Agriculture*:

> (The) Women's Institute is for all alike; rich and poor ... learned and unlearned – all pay the same subscription, have the same privileges and the same responsibilities. Each member in turn acts as hostess to her fellow members; each puts her own practical knowledge at the service of the rest. Controversial subjects: religious or

political are taboo; but interest in their own homes tends naturally and inevitably to interest in questions of housing, sanitation, infant welfare and kindred topics. The members learn to realise their responsibility towards the community in which they live, and, from an interest in their own village and their own country, come to see the connection between their affairs and those of the nation at large. It would be difficult to plan a better training for the exercise of the vote ...

Miss Evelyn Lamport who had been president, and Mrs. Charlotte Price White who had been secretary, of by far the largest and most active NUWSS in North Wales at Bangor, became founder members of the Executive Council of North Wales WI's.

The first WI in Britain was founded at Llanfairpwll on the Island of Anglesey on **16 September 1915** as the result of a visit by Mrs. Madge Watt, under the auspices of the Agricultural Organisation Society (AOS). This body had been set up by the government at the beginning of WW1 to advise on food production. Mrs. Watt's brief was to spread the gospel of the WI in Britain.

The WI had its roots in Canada. When the youngest child of Mrs. Adelaide Hoodless died from:

the summer complaint

contracted by drinking contaminated milk delivered in open churns, she decided that young women must be educated about hygiene. Her first, hard fought campaign was eventually successful in getting domestic science onto the curriculum in Ontario schools. In December 1896 she was invited to speak at the Ontario Agricultural College. One of the farmers present that night, Mr. Erland Lee, was so impressed by what Mrs. Hoodless had to say and the way she said it, that he invited her to speak at a meeting of the Farmer's Institute in his village, Stoney Creek, the following February. Not all the farmers were happy at the prospect of a woman speaker, but they turned up – along with thirty-five of their wives. Mrs. Hoodless spoke of the importance of a sound knowledge of domestic science, not

Adelaide Hoodless, founder WI Canada

just for growing girls – but for women like themselves too. She sympathised with them – she had been brought up on a farm and knew it could be a hard and lonely life. And then she made a suggestion – the men had their Institute, why shouldn't the women have one as well, where they could learn both from visiting speakers and each-other? Mr. Lee asked for a show of hands of women who would be interested and thirty-five hands shot up!

One week later, at the height of a storm, Mr. Lee, Mrs. Hoodless and a hundred and one other women turned up at the Farmer's Institute, and what became the Women's Institute of Stoney Creek was formed.

In 1913 several Canadian women, including Mrs. Madge Watt came to Britain to try to introduce the movement here, but without success. At the invitation of Mr. John Nugent Harris, secretary of the AOS, Mrs. Watt joined the organisation. Mr. Nugent Harris had been trying to set up

Madge Watt, AOS/WI

something similar to the WI for several years but had also failed. He engineered an invitation for Mrs. Watt to address the North Wales branch of the AOS at University College North Wales (UCNW), Bangor. So impressed was the chairman, Colonel Richard Stapleton-Cotton, that he invited a group of women from his home village, Llanfairpwll, to meet Mrs. Watt to consider the possibility of forming a WI. The Colonel was well known for his tireless efforts to benefit the community and so the women were eager to meet her. From Mrs. Watt's point of view he was an unlikely ally – she hadn't much time for the gentry.

The report in the *North Wales Chronicle* for **18 June 1915** read:

A well attended meeting, presided over by Col. Stapleton-Cotton, was held at Graig, by permission of Mrs. W.E. Jones, on Wednesday. The lecturer was Mrs. Watt, a lady from British Columbia, who gave an interesting account of the work done in that portion of the Empire by means of the WI. It was proposed by Mrs. J.G. Wilson and seconded by Miss Watts, that a society of this description be established in the village. The motion was passed unanimously.

When I asked if it was possible to obtain copies of the early minutes of Llanfairpwll WI, I was directed to *A Grain of Mustard Seed* (a biblical reference to the smallest seed growing into the largest herb) written by Constance Davies. I am indebted to Mrs. Davies for collating the information concerning both the committees and members meetings. Not all meetings are included and I can only conclude that those most worthy of note were chosen. I, in turn, have selected only the most interesting accounts.

On **11 September** an open meeting was held in the drawing room at Graig when a committee was formed. The Hon. Mrs. Jane Stapleton-Cotton was elected president, and such was the affection in which her husband was held, that he and his dog, Tinker became the only two male paid-up members of the WI – ever! The vice-president and treasurer was Mrs. W.E. Jones (Graig), the secretary Mrs. J.G. Wilson (Florence) and the committee comprised: Mrs. Edwards (Tyddyn Fadog), Mrs. Jones (Bron Llwyn), Mrs. J. Morris-Jones (Ty Coch), Miss B. Prichard (Menai House), Miss Roberts (Post Office), Miss Watts (Aberbraint) and Mrs. J.R. Williams (Tremarfon).

The next meeting was on **16 September** and was attended by Mrs. Watt (AOS) who spoke about the objects of the WI movement. At this meeting the following resolutions were put to the meeting and carried:

> That they should form a WI in Llanfairpwll affiliated to the AOS
> That it be called Llanfairpwll Women's Institute
> That regular monthly meetings of an educational and social character, be held at 2 pm on the first Tuesday of each month in the Summerhouse at Graig kindly lent by Mrs. W.E. Jones until such time as the WI has its own building

That the membership fee of 2/- be paid in advance at the annual meeting, to be held in January of each year
That new members be proposed by an existing member and
That members should not be confined to Llanfairpwll parish.

The Summerhouse at Graig, Llanfairpwll WI's first 'home'

And so began the traditional format of business, a talk or demonstration by a visiting speaker or occasionally, contributions by the WI's own members; followed by the opportunity to chat over tea and homemade cake. But from the outset the WI encouraged women to broaden their horizons both practically and academically.

Not letting the grass grow under their feet, on **21 September** the committee met, and again, Mrs. Watt (AOS) attended. The following resolutions were put to the meeting and carried:

That food supply of the country be the special subject for discussion (bearing in mind that this was wartime and the food supply, particularly in the towns, was precarious)

That the day of the regular meeting should be the third Tuesday in each month and that the first meeting be held on 25 September

That gifts towards the furnishing of the room would be received at the next meeting

That tea, bread and one kind of cake be served at each meeting. Tea and sugar would be supplied by the WI. Two or more members to supply the food.

On 25 September the meeting to launch the WI was held. Mrs. Watt (AOS) spoke on *Fruit and Vegetable Preserving*. Miss A. Thomas played the harp, the Welsh and English National Anthems were sung, and tea was provided by Mrs. Cotton and Mrs. W.E. Jones. Three wounded soldiers were guests.

19 October, WI Meeting

There was a discussion about the aims of the WI. It was stressed that it was un-denominational and un-political. Members felt that their aim should to be to foster a spirit of unselfishness and help one another. And they believed the fact that theirs was the first WI in Britain should spur them on.

Mrs. W.E. Jones demonstrated the fireless cooker. This was a hay box, where a covered container of food in hot liquid e.g. stew, was placed inside a box of hay. The heat generated from the container was retained by the hay, and the food continued to cook – the first slow cooker.

Gifts of crockery for the Summerhouse were gratefully received.

Col. Cotton issued an invitation to members to visit his

autumn garden at Plas Llwynonn the following week, which many ladies accepted. They thoroughly enjoyed their visit and learned a lot through both observation and practical experience. Mrs. Cotton entertained them to tea.

8 November Committee

It was decided that recitations must be eliminated from future meetings!

Mrs. Morris-Jones was thanked for tea-cloths and Miss Watts for tablecloths.

14 December, WI Meeting

This was a purely social event with games and singing etc. Each member was asked to bring their husband or a man friend. Refreshments were provided by members in abundance (despite the war!) and the surplus was sold for WI funds.

1916
11 January WI AGM

Mrs. Cotton reported on what had happened so far. Mrs. Nugent Harris, Mrs. E. Jones and Mrs. Watt: all from the AOS emphasised the importance of food production and the significance of the WI with regard to this.

Many new members enrolled and everyone was invited to tea. Being January, we can imagine how grateful they were for Col. Cotton's timely gift of an oil cooking stove.

15 January Committee

It was proposed that they should have a badge based on the Canadian design, but with the dragon or leek in red and gold; the inscription to be: *Fy nwglad, A'm cartref* (My country, My home).

16 March WI Meeting

Col. Cotton spoke (at length!) about *Women's Labour on the Land*, and it was decided that a poll of the village should be taken regarding potential help.

A bread-making demonstration was given by Mrs. Clegg and the results were eaten for tea.

(un-dated) **April WI Meeting**

Mrs. Cotton invited members to tea. Although it was a cold, wet day the welcome was warm, and they enjoyed seeing the Daffodils and other spring flowers through the windows. Mrs. Cotton was also thanked for the car – which presumably relayed them to and from Plas Llwynonn.

16 May WI Meeting

Mrs. Hunter-Smith **demonstrated** *The Easiest and Most Humane Way of Killing a Fowl.* She also spoke about how to prepare and dress it, to increase its marketable value.

19 September Committee

It was proposed that a War Loan Association be formed in connection with the WI, also that a Suggestion Box should be available at meetings.

This was immediately followed by the:

WI's 1st Birthday Meeting

Col. Cotton announced that his birthday gift was £150 to open the Building Fund. This, predictably, caused a lot of excitement.

29 September Extraordinary Meeting

Miss Talbot and Miss La Mothe from the Board of Agriculture and Fisheries (BOAF) interviewed members of the committee about the viability of forming further WI's.

27 October Committee

This meeting was to consider War Loans. It was proposed that Mr. J.G. Wilson be secretary and Mrs. Ross treasurer, and that a speaker on the subject should be invited in November.

It was also decided to have a table at meetings for hand-made items and produce, and that a proportion of the sale price should be donated to WI funds. (There were constant reminders about this because it was not generally very well supported, but occasionally there was a bumper crop).

8 November Committee

Mrs. Wilson explained that since the decision had been taken to have a badge, correspondence had ensued, but there seemed to be a difficulty with regard to the labour entailed in making them. It was therefore finally decided not to have badges – it being most unpatriotic at the present time etc. She added:

The needs of our beloved country should come first.

(Mrs. Wilson was very fond of *etc* – occasionally even *etc., etc., etc!*)

18 November WI Meeting

Mr. W. Jones, Llangefni, explained clearly how to form and maintain a War Savings Association. (The government needed investment to fund the war, and offered bonds which were expected to be repaid with 4% interest 1925-1928. This was considered to be very attractive as well as patriotic, but unfortunately was not as well supported as had been hoped. Only about half of the 350 million bonds on offer were actually bought by the general public). Thirty-three names and subscriptions were collected, which was considered very gratifying.

15 December Committee

The possibility of affiliating the newly formed WI's War Savings Association to one for the whole village was discussed. It was decided to call a public meeting and invite special speakers.

A letter from the AOS asking the WI to accept the gift of a chiming clock was read by Mrs. Wilson. This was received with pleasure. (Maybe someone from the AOS had been present when Col Cotton spoke – at length, at the March meeting!)

The **1915-16 Annual Report** contained the information that a fruit and vegetable sterilizer had been donated by the late Mr. R.A. Yerburgh – so now they could have jam as well as *Jeruslem*!

1917
16 February WI Meeting
Dr. Williams spoke at length about a *Maternity and Nursing Scheme.* (Obviously the chiming clock was not having the desired effect).

It was reported that the WI had held a Social Evening and sold forty-six tickets at 1/- in order to help the Red Cross Committee pay two unexpected bills. The WI felt gratified to have been able to help the Red Cross.

20 April WI Meeting
Dr. Price from Bangor spoke forcibly on *The Dangers of Flies in Rubbish Heaps.*

15 May WI Meeting
Members enjoyed another very pleasant visit to Plas Llwynonn.

19 June WI Meeting
Mrs. Charlotte Price White (who had been the Bangor NUWSS secretary and became chairman of the North Wales Women's Peace Council) spoke (again at length) on: *Food: its value as an asset in the future, with regard to the welfare of the individual and the community.*

(Un-dated) July WI Meeting
This meeting was attended by Mrs. Watt (AOS) and took the form of an informal conversation. It was felt that a lot of information which would be very helpful in the future had been forth-coming.

(Un-dated) August WI Meeting
Members were entertained by Lady Anglesey at Plas Newydd.

Convalescent soldiers at Bodlondeb Red Cross Military Hospital

18 September WI Meeting
The WI ladies invited forty-eight soldiers and nurses from Bodlondeb Red Cross Military Hospital in Bangor to sports and tea and gave them

A royal time.

27 September Special WI Meeting: Girls' Club
It was proposed that a Girl's Club for over fourteens be formed in the village and that it should meet each Tuesday 6-8.30 pm. Presumably it was to be held at the Council School, as Miss Williams was instructed to write to the school managers to request the use of the kitchen. Three or four WI ladies would need to be responsible for each meeting.

9 October Special WI Meeting: Girls' Club
It was decided that the Girl's Club opening night would be on 16 October; and to give the girls tea and bread and butter. Mrs. Roberts, Caretaker, to light fires, lamps etc. and be paid 1/- per week.

16 October Opening of Girl's Club

Thirty-two girls were present, twenty-four of whom paid the full 1/- fee for the whole session (they could pay by instalments if they wished). Twenty-one WI members attended. It was pointed out that the Club would continue to need both material and physical help to ensure its success. Tea was provided by the WI at a cost of 7/10d.

23 October WI Meeting

The WI was no longer affiliated to the AOS and now came under the auspices of the Board of Agriculture and Fisheries (BOAF).

20 November WI Meeting

This was an experimental meeting – no speaker was booked, but it proved very successful and it was very much hoped that it would be repeated.

The **1917 Annual Report** recorded a donation of £100 to the Building Fund from Mrs. Clegg.

Heartiest congratulations were proffered to Mrs. W.E. Jones on her appointment as WI Organiser and to Lady Morris-Jones on the Knighthood conferred upon her husband. There was further good news in that a nurse had been obtained for the village.

After due consideration, it was decided by the committee to continue with tea at monthly meetings – keeping strictly to the rationing orders.

The events leading up to Mrs. W.E. Jones becoming County Organiser are worthy of record. In their infinite wisdom, BOAF, under whose remit the WI's now came, appointed a non Welsh-speaker as County Organiser for Anglesey and Caernarfonshire. Her job was to support existing Institutes and set up new ones; but this proved impossible for her in remote rural villages where the women's first, and sometimes only language, was Welsh. An un-named woman then complained to BOAF that the WI's were undemocratic! This led, in due course, to the formation of the self-governing North Wales Union of Women's Institutes (NWUWI) and Welsh-speaking Mrs. W.E. Jones' appointment.

28 December Committee held at Col. Cotton's Bulb Farm. It was proposed that a piano costing £10 be bought for the Girl's Club.

1918

19 February WI Meeting

Miss Griffiths (Col. and Mrs. Cotton's cook), at very short notice and under great difficulties, demonstrated a few simple dishes.

19 March WI Meeting

Professor Phillips of UCNW gave a short talk on *The Gathering of Wild Herbs for Medicinal Purposes.* This fired the imagination of the ladies who were eager to be up and at it, but following a stern rebuke from the professor, who left them in no doubt that **nothing** should sidetrack them from food production, they agreed to leave it for the present.

(Un-dated) **April WI Discussion Meeting** at Aberbraint

It was proposed:

That Col. Cotton be asked to draw up a resolution emanating from the WI, to be submitted to Llangefni County Council as to whether it would be possible to have some (sort of) water scheme for Llanfairpwll

That they hold a Baby Day

That a sub-committee be formed for the purpose of organising regular needlework meetings

That recipes should be collected by Mrs. Green and Mrs. Langland with a view to publishing a WI cookery book

That Mrs. R.W. Roberts, Mrs. Ross and Miss Williams (Min-y-Don) organise a regular literature table and magazine club.

Miss Watts was thanked for the use of Aberbraint, the Summerhouse at Graig being unavailable on this occasion.

18 June WI Meeting

Mrs. Dr. Williams spoke about a meeting at UCNW on *The Housing Question* and a letter from Lady Sarah Hughes-Hunter on the same subject was read.

There followed a most interesting talk by Miss Goodwin on Home Remedies.

29 July WI Meeting

Mrs. Watt (AOS) and members of the Summer School for WI Organisers which was being held at UCNW attended. Mrs. W.E. Jones had invited them to lunch, after which they had visited the gardens at Plas Newydd and the Bulb Farm.

Miss Lamport spoke on *The Home Beautiful*.

On behalf of herself and her guests, Mrs. Watt thanked the WI for their invitation, and assured them that she would always have a special interest in Llanfairpwll due to it being the first WI in Britain.

The afternoon ended with tea and everyone agreed how pleasant it was to have been able to hold this meeting out of doors due to the fine weather.

15 October WI Meeting

The members were very disappointed that Mr. Ffoulkes Price White (Manager of Bangor Electricity Station which had opened in 1901), who was to have spoken on *The Fuel Question* was unable to do so, due to having Influenza.

(**November WI meeting** cancelled in view of Influenza epidemic).

31 December Christmas Party.

Between ninety and a hundred people – members accompanied by their husband, male friend or brother, accepted the invitation to attend the party at the Council School. The Garden Girls (Land Girls) stationed at Plas Newydd, who took a great interest in the WI, were also invited and joined in with great enthusiasm.

1919

21 January WI AGM

The question of badges was finally settled in their favour and the secretary, Mrs. Wilson, was instructed to order them at 1/1d each.

She then begged leave to resign but was over-ruled, and consented to continue with the help of an assistant, namely Mrs. Defferd.

At this point a proposal was taken from the Suggestion Box which caused animated discussion, was put to the vote and carried unanimously – but unfortunately it is not known what the proposal was!

18 February WI Meeting

A letter from Mrs. Sotheby was read thanking the WI for its donation of £5-13-4d (raised by a Whist Drive) towards reducing the debt on the YMCA hut.

The secretary was empowered to buy a brush, cedar mop, dish-cloth and washing-up bowl.

It was proposed that Miss A. Williams' suggestion concerning a Dispenser should be sent to Dr. Williams. There was a second proposal to secure the services of a Dispenser at Mrs. Thomas' twice per week.

Mrs. Defferd, Mrs. W.E. Jones (Graig) and Mrs. Williams (Ty Hen) were deputed to attend at the District Council with a view to trying to arrange a water supply for the village and to protest about the present state of drainage.

Notice was given that an exhibition of work and produce from all the WI's in the NWUWI, was to be held at Caernarfon in July or September (dependent on date of London Exhibition). Afterwards exhibits were to be collected by Criccieth members and sent on to London.

The sum of £2-10/- surplus from a working party, started in 1914, which had provided (knitted) comforts for soldiers, was to be expended on an evening's entertainment for local men home from the front. This was to take place at once and any excess cost was to be defrayed by the WI.

Notice was also given that a Roll Call would be brought into force at next meeting!

Mrs. Hawkey was unable to come to demonstrate *Rational Dressmaking* but Mrs. Luther Jones saved the day with *How to make Chamois Leather Gloves.*

7 March Committee at the Bulb Farm

A vote of sympathy was expressed to Col. and Mrs. Cotton on the death of their daughter, Lady Hood.

18 March WI Meeting

Miss Goodwin spoke on *Ordinary Rules of Life appertaining to Health, in relation to Spring Cleaning and House Furnishing.*

A deputation of men from the Memorial Institute attended, to discuss the proposed War Memorial Hall. The WI was to have a wing for its exclusive use, but the ladies favoured further discussion before committing themselves.

The Roll was called but unfortunately very few members responded with recipes.

(Un-dated) **WI Party for returned servicemen**

This was held at the Council School and took the form of a Whist Drive organised by Mr. and Mrs. Green. Seventy servicemen and forty-five WI members attended. Nearly every serviceman won some sort of prize and it was considered to have been a most enjoyable evening.

15 April WI Meeting

Mrs. W.E. Jones gave details of a meeting of the site committee for the new War Memorial Hall. Members voted unanimously in favour of the Toll Gate House site. This decision was to be conveyed to the men on the site committee.

Miss Daisy Price from Bangor spoke on: *Bolshevism in its Simplest Form.*

The Toll Gate House

(Un-dated) **July WI Meeting**
This meeting took the form of a Baby Show but unfortunately the report has been lost.

The WI had been approached by the Parish Council to organise the refreshments for the Peace Day celebrations, which was done most satisfactorily with the help of non-members. The Parish Council had paid tribute to the organising power of the WI.

4 September WI Meeting
In response to an appeal made to WI's throughout Britain by St. Dunstan's Home for Blinded Soldiers, Mrs. Horridge kindly held a small garden party at her home. Admission was 1/6d including tea – which included everything that could be desired! An un-named, but very talented little girl danced, recited and sang. The total raised was £12-11/-.

2 October Committee at the Bulb Farm
For the first time, those present were recorded: Mrs. Defferd, Lady Morris-Jones, Mrs. W.E. Jones, Mrs. Ross, Mrs. Rowlands, Miss Watts and Mrs. Wilson.

Mrs. W.E. Jones explained that although the County Council had not looked favourably upon the Water Scheme request, if the Marquess of Anglesey's Water Scheme went ahead, the council would be willing to try to obtain benefits for Llanfairpwll from that, should the Marquess be willing.

It was recommended that the WI pay rent for the Toll Gate House in order for it to be used as a clinic, committee room etc., but approval was to be sought from members. (In fact the 6th Marquess allowed the WI to use it rent-free for over twenty-five years).

Mrs. Cotton provided tea at the end of the meeting.

16 December WI Meeting

A letter was read from Lady Denman, WI National Chairman suggesting an increase of 6d on member's affiliation fees: 3d for HQ and 3d for the County Federation. A protest was made that this was exorbitant!

1920

20 January WI AGM

Once again Mrs. Wilson begged leave to resign as secretary: but was over-ruled and consented to continue with the help of an assistant, namely Mrs. Williams (Ty Hen).

The War Savings Association had been wound up, £3,234-7-3d having been collected up to end of 1919.

The announcement of a gift of £500 to the Building Fund generated prolonged applause. (It is not clear who the gift came from).

Mrs. W.E. Jones, secretary of the War Memorial Institute Committee reported that the site chosen was Y Ffordd Deg. Discussion followed about whether the WI was taking undue advantage of Mrs. W.E. Jones' generosity in giving it the use of the Summerhouse at Graig for a further indefinite, probably prolonged, period. Mrs. Jones refuted this, so the WI decided to avail itself of her continued kindness.

Mrs. Sotheby brought articles vertu (objets d'art – usually Italian) for sale in aid of a prospective club. (It is not clear what this was).

17 February WI Meeting

Mrs. Cotton spoke on: *The Need for an Isolation Hospital.* It was proposed that Mr. W.O. Jones, Llangefni, be approached concerning Gwalchmai Aerodrome, as being a suitable place.

Mrs. Wilson explained the intentions of the WI concerning the running of the Clinic.

17 April Committee at the Clinic Rooms.

It was recommended that the WI room be cleaned every month – by a woman!

20 May, Whit Tuesday WI Meeting

On behalf of WI members, Mrs. Cotton presented secretary, Mr. J.G. Wilson, and treasurer, Mrs. Ross, of the War Savings Association, with a writing-case and a handbag respectively.

17 June Garden Party

This was held at Graig, admission was 1/6d including tea: consisting of sandwiches, salad, bread and butter, and currant bread. Unfortunately a bad thunderstorm marred the afternoon, tables and chairs had to be hurriedly brought indoors and the room was very crowded – but everyone was amiable.

There was a stall of saleable items: cakes, eggs, flowers, fruit, vegetables and virtually anything deemed useful. There was also a guessing the weight of a cake competition. And members of Newborough WI brought a basket of novelties for sale, which was a great success.

The total raised was £11-10/- of which £10 was sent to HQ.

20 July WI Meeting

Miss Lamport spoke and offended a lot of people! She

referred to *Reincarnation* which apparently contravened the non-sectarian rule (the other being non-political). More care was to be taken when allowing speakers to choose their own subjects in future.

9 August Committee at the Clinic Rooms

Mrs. Nugent Harris from WI HQ explained the new rules and offered advice on how to keep them.

It was resolved that the cost of membership would remain at 2/- but there would be no reduction for additional family members.

Discussion ensued concerning the inadequacy of the Toll Gate House, resulting in Col. Cotton being asked for advice and help in procuring an annexe. He promised to view a hut which he knew was coming up for sale soon.

August

A much needed holiday!

29 September

About forty-three members were photographed by Mr. Watts of St. Asaph, followed by coffee and sandwiches which were appreciated by all. Cost to WI: 13/9d. A bright interlude!

Early members of Llanfairpwll WI

20 October WI Meeting

Discussion continued concerning buying a hut, but it was decided to wait until January. Col. Cotton promised to donate £200 towards the cost.

Mr. Defferd spoke on *The Aims of the newly formed Village Clubs Association.*

16 November WI Meeting

Mrs. W.E. Jones reported on her visit to Kinmel Park to view huts. Animated discussion followed about what was required, but it was agreed that nothing further could be done until Col. Cotton had received a reply to his enquiry.

30 November Committee at the Clinic Rooms

It was proposed that Col. Cotton and Mr. and Mrs. W.E. Jones should attend the sale at Kinmel Park and be empowered to spend upwards of £120

3 December Committee at the Clinic Rooms

Concerning the Kinmel Park Sale: Col. Cotton was indisposed and Mr. W.E. Jones was also unable to attend. Lieutenant Jones, secretary of the Village Clubs Association, together with Mrs. W.E. Jones bought an Officer's Mess for £140 and a boiler for £2. (Mrs. Jones being willing to take latter if not required).

14 December WI Meeting

The Building Committee was formed, secretary: Mrs. Green. Lively discussion followed concerning tenders for the removal of the hut from Kinmel Park and fixing of same at Llanfairpwll.

21 December Clinic Meeting

The clinic committee and helpers organised a Christmas Tree for the mothers and babies; who in turn presented Nurse Williams with a handbag and thermometer in gratitude for all her sympathetic help. Thanks were also expressed to the secretary, treasurer and helpers.

1921

(Un-dated) **January WI AGM**

Mrs. Green gave a brief resume of the work of the building committee. The suggestion to issue shares to WI members, had not appealed to the majority of those present at the meeting where it had been proposed. However, when Mrs. Wilson approached members individually £72-7-6d was promised immediately! It was therefore proposed that Mrs. Wilson become treasurer of Building Fund, with help from Mrs. Williams (Ty Hen). The list of promises was read, punctuated with applause. Mrs. Cotton promised further financial support from herself and her husband.

15 February WI Meeting

Due to a Military Funeral in the village the intended programme was shortened.

Mrs. Dorothy Drage from Criccieth spoke on *The History of Lace Making* and showed examples. It was hoped that a lace-making group could be formed in Llanfairpwll.

After the funeral, the WI provided hospitality for fifteen nurses from Holyhead who had attended.

1 March, St. David's Day, Joint Committee and Building Committee Meeting at the Bulb Farm

Mr. [*sic*] Nugent Harris (AOS) was nominated as the Representative of Llanfairpwll WI on the Executive Committee of the National Federation of Women's Institutes (NFWI).

There was discussion about appointing a caretaker for the new extension. Several unsolicited applications had already been received, but it was decided to wait for a few months before employing anyone.

5 April (Bazaar) Committee at Graig

It was decided to hold a Sale of Work at 3 pm on 4 May, to be opened by Lady Anglesey if possible: Mrs. Cotton was to approach her.

It was proposed by Mrs. Rowlands (Shop) that admission should be 1/- to include tea: consisting of bread and butter and a scone (cakes extra). Helpers in whatever capacity were to pay the admission fee!

There would be the following stalls: Bran Tub/Lucky Dip: Mrs. Jones, Mrs. Ollosson; Cakes and Sweets: Mrs. Cotton, Lady Morris-Jones; Crockery Ornaments: Mrs. Wilson; Domestic items: Mrs. W.E. Jones; Fancy goods: Mrs. Green; Flowers: Miss Watts; 1 lb. stall (everything weighed one pound): Mrs. Holbrook and the Girls Club; and Thrift Garments: Nurse Williams. Refreshments: Miss Donnithorne, Miss Owen, Mrs. Rowlands (Bron Llwyn) and Mrs. Rowlands (Shop). The Girl Guides were to be asked to give a short display and Mrs. Hughes-Williams asked to sing. Flowers were to be presented to Mrs. Cotton and Lady Anglesey.

The date was changed to 2 June.

19 April WI Meeting

On behalf of the WI, Mrs. Cotton thanked Mrs. W.E. Jones for the use of the Summerhouse at Graig (with fires), since August 1914. She commented that there was always sadness when saying *Goodbye* – they had always felt at home at the Summerhouse and had spent many happy hours there. She hoped they would carry the same spirit into their new home.

A vote of thanks was accorded to Col. Cotton for a new Minute Book:

a very handsome volume.

This seems an appropriate time to leave the regular reports, but I do want to mention just a few items from the new Minute Book:

6 May Committee

In addition to the above, the following arrangements were made for the forthcoming bazaar:

Each stall holder was to be responsible for supplying £1 in change and recruiting helpers; treasurers for stalls to be: Cakes and Sweets: Miss O. Matthews; Crockery Ornaments: Mrs. Sargent; Domestic items: Mrs. Furneaux; Fancy goods: Mrs. R.W. Roberts; Flowers: Miss Lydia Owen; and 1 lb. stall: Miss Maggie Jones. Mr. Defferd was to be asked to count the takings at the end.

The following items were promised for the teas: Mrs. Owen (Carregddyfnallt): 2 lbs butter, milk and cakes; Mrs. Owen (Parsonage): sandwich cake; Mrs. Thomas (Garnedd): 2 lbs butter, milk and cakes; Miss Watts: cakes; Miss Williams (Min y Don): 2 lbs tea; and Mrs. Wilson: cakes.

20 May Committee at the Clinic Rooms

The committee was warned that in order to avoid Entertainment Tax **NO** expense must be incurred. Teas were to be served 3-5 pm, after that there would be a charge of 6d.

Mrs. O. Roberts offered to defray the cost of printing tickets, and Miss Essie Jones agreed to type some hand-bills for advertising purposes. There would be no flowers for Mrs. Cotton and Lady Anglesey as the expense would have incurred tax! The bazaar raised £134-11-2½d.

1924

August: the Death of Mrs. Cotton

A wire of sympathy was sent at once to Col. Cotton by Mrs. Wilson.

A Memorial Service was held at St. Mary's Church, Menai Bridge, which many members attended. A wreath made by members was sent from the WI.

This is an appreciation of Mrs. Cotton sent to *Home and Country* (the WI magazine) by Mrs. W.E. Jones:

In the death of Mrs. R. Stapleton-Cotton, Craig-yr-Halen, Menai Bridge, Llanfairpwll WI has lost its beloved president, and the National Federation has lost the worker who, with her husband, organised the meeting at which the first Women's Institute was started in England and Wales. Llanfairpwll has had Mrs. Cotton as president ever since. She was a member of the first Executive Committee of the NFWI and while her health permitted attended meetings in London. Mrs. Cotton won the love of all who knew her. Her kindness and unselfishness will never be forgotten. It must mean something that the first president of the first WI had a spirit abounding in the beauty of Christian charity. The influence of her goodness will abide. Every WI will wish to extend its sympathy to Col. Cotton, one of the earliest and best friends of the Movement.

1925
November: the Death of Colonel Cotton
We record with regret the passing away of Colonel Cotton in the West Indies. He was:

> a good friend to us, always.

1935
17 September: the Twentieth Birthday Party
Nearly 500 WI members from all over Great Britain attended Llanfairpwll's Twentieth Birthday Party, and there were also representatives from Canada – Miss Oxner and New Zealand – Mrs. Irving. The party was held outside the Summerhouse at Graig where the very first meeting had been held. The following founder members were present: Mrs. Cross, Mrs. Green, Lady Morris-Jones, Mrs. W.E. Jones, Mrs. Parry, Mrs. Pretty, Mrs. Pritchard (Ty Gwyn,

Gaerwen), Mrs. Prytherch, Miss Watts and Mrs. Williams (Ty Hen).

Miss Davies JP OBE president of the Anglesey Federation said how proud they were that the first WI in Great Britain had started in this little village.

Mr. Nugent Harris (AOS) spoke about the history of the WI and particularly mentioned Col. and Mrs. Cotton, whom he had known personally. He also paid tribute to Mrs. and the late Mr. W.E. Jones for their kindness and generosity in placing The Summerhouse at the disposal of the WI for as long as they needed it – which had turned out to be nearly seven years. He stated that the WI was a wonderful power for uniting all classes of women to work for the good of their communities.

The meeting closed with the Welsh and English National Anthems, accompanied on the harp by Mrs. Evans of Bethesda.

Tea, which included an enormous three-tier birthday cake topped with a model of The Summerhouse, was served in the WI's hall.

A year later, one month after the WI's Twenty-First Birthday, Mrs. W.E. Jones died.

I am so pleased to report that as I write, in autumn 2019, Llanfairpwll WI still meets at 2 pm on the third Tuesday of the month.

Composer, Sir Hubert Parry, gave the rights to *Jerusalem* to Millicent Fawcett's law-abiding NUWSS in 1918. When the NUWSS was finally wound-up in 1928 (the year women under thirty got the vote), Parry's executors re-assigned the rights to the WI. More than a century later they are still striving, through education, campaigning for what they believe in, friendship – and fun, to build the *new Jerusalem* for country women in Britain.

Llanfairpwll Women's Institute
Who was Who

The **primary source** of information is the 1911 Census and where ages are given they are the ages in that year. If I have been unable to trace people in 1911 I have looked at the 1901 Census and again, where ages are given they are the ages in that year.

I have also used Gwynedd Family History Society's *Memorial Inscriptions at the Church of St. Mary, Llanfair Pwllgwyngyll, Anglesey.*

Note: Mrs. Bella Clegg, Col. and Mrs. Stapleton-Cotton, Lady Hughes-Hunter, and Lady Gwen Neave supported many of the same causes. Therefore I have included only the first account of each event, if more than one of them attended.

FM: Founder Member **Biography at the end of this section

Officers and Committee Members:

Lady ANGLESEY, (Victoria) **Marjorie Harriet Paget
**Mrs. (Rebecca) Bella CLEGG
**Col. Hon. Richard Southwell George Stapleton-COTTON (FM)

**Hon. Mrs. Jane Charlotte Stapleton-COTTON (FM)
**Tinker Stapleton-COTTON (FM)
Mrs. Ellen DEFFERD acted as assistant-secretary from 1919 and was a member of the deputation to the District Council to request a water supply to the village.
Mrs. EDWARDS (Tyddyn Fadog) (FM) was a member of the original committee.
Miss Edwen EDWARDS (Tyddyn Fadog) married and became **Mrs. Christopher Hughes**. At the time *A Grain of Mustard Seed* was written (1954) she was Secretary, and described as:

the most truly loved member of the Institute.

Mrs. GREEN (FM) was asked to collect recipes for the WI cookery book, joined the committee in 1920 and became secretary of the Building Fund in 1921.

Mrs. W.E. JONES (FM) was the wife of the County Surveyor and 6th Marquess' estate Agent. The very first WI meeting was held in her home, Graig, and her Summerhouse is now world famous as the place where Llanfairpwll WI met for its first six years. Mrs. Jones was vice-president and treasurer from the outset. She was a member of the deputation to the

Mrs. W.E. Jones

District Council to request a water supply to the village. In 1920 she became the press correspondent. After the death of Mrs. Cotton and the illness of both Mrs. Mansell-Morgan and Mrs. Llewelyn Mansell-Morgan, Mrs. Jones became president in 1927. She was also North Wales Organiser for the WI.

Despite the recent death of her husband and her own failing health, in September 1935 she was delighted to welcome the huge crowd which assembled to celebrate the WI's twentieth birthday; and she lived just long enough to attend its coming of age party the following year. She died a month later, in October 1936.

Mrs. JONES (Bron Llwyn) (FM) was a member of the original committee.

Mrs. JONES (Madryn House) joined the committee in 1920.

Lady John Morris-JONES (Mary) (Ty Coch) (FM) was a member of the original committee. Her husband, John, was a lecturer in Welsh at UCNW and was knighted in 1918. They had four daughters. She became president after the death of Mrs. W.E. Jones and introduced what became the tradition, of holding the March (St. David's Day) meeting entirely in Welsh. She died in 1948 and is buried with her husband in St. Mary's Churchyard, Llanfairpwll.

Mrs. Annie LANGLANDS (twenty-nine) was asked to collect recipes for the WI cookery book and acted as assistant-secretary from the beginning of 1918. In the 1911 Census she lived at 2 Alma Terrace with her son David (five) and twin daughters Elspeth and Maria (two), before leaving to live in London towards the end of 1918. At some point she returned to Anglesey, she died in 1946 and is buried with her husband, William, in St. Mary's Churchyard, Llanfairpwll.

**Mrs. Mansell-MORGAN

Mrs. Llewelyn (Elenor) Mansell-MORGAN, (nèe Clifford Hughes) was the daughter of Sir Frederick and Lady Hughes of Baintown House, Wexford, Eire. She married Llewelyn, the youngest son of Captain and Mrs. Mansell-Morgan.

She was president of Llanfairpwll WI for a short time, until ill health forced her to resign.

Mrs. PARRY (FM) was a member of the original committee.

Miss Blodwen PRICHARD (Menai House) (FM) was a member of the original committee.

Miss ROBERTS (Post Office) (FM) was a member of the original committee.

Miss Roberts' Llanfairpwll Post Office

Mrs. ROSS was a committee member and War Savings treasurer from 1916. With others she ran the magazine club from 1918, and served as the Anglesey representative on NWUWI until 1919. She left Anglesey in 1920.

Mrs. ROWLANDS (Bron Llwyn) joined the committee in 1919 and became treasurer in 1921.

Mrs. Ellen ROWLANDS (forty-six) lived at Bryn Goleu, with her husband Thomas (fifty) bridge painter, sons Edward (thirteen), Madoc (six), daughter Mary Jane (eleven) and aunt Ellen Stuart, widow (eighty-six). Mrs. Rowlands joined the committee in 1920.

Mrs. TAYLOR joined the committee in 1920.

Mrs. Captain THOMAS joined the committee in 1917.

Miss Sarah WATTS (FM) (forty-seven) lived at Aberbraint, Llanedwen with her brother, George (forty-five) boarding house keeper, they employed a cook and house maid. Miss Watts was a member of the original committee.

Miss Watts's Aberbraint Guesthouse

Mrs. John WILLIAMS joined the committee in 1917.

Mrs. J.R. WILLIAMS (Tremarfon) (FM) was a member of the original committee.

Mrs. WILLIAMS (Ty Hen) (FM) was a member of the deputation to the District Council to request a water supply to village, assistant-secretary from 1920 and assistant-treasurer of the building fund from 1921.

Mrs. J.G. WILSON (Florence) (FM) (forty-four) lived with her husband, James (forty-six) relay clerk, at 3 Britannia Terrace. She was the original secretary, and treasurer of the building fund from 1921. As can be deduced from the brief but accurate minutes, Mrs. Wilson was a down-to-earth Yorkshire-woman, not given to wasting words. But her Minute on Col. Cotton's death:

> He was a good friend to us, always

surely reveals a warm heart. She tried to resign as secretary twice, but was not allowed to do so. Eventually she returned home to Yorkshire.

Known Members Sept. 1915 – Apr. 21

(there were many more – the 1917 Annual Report stated that they had seventy members, but these are names mentioned in the minutes):

Mrs. Elizabeth CROSS, (forty) (FM) lived at Maen Afon with her husband, William (forty) signalman, and daughter, Ellen (fourteen). Mrs. Cross died in 1962 and is buried with her husband in St. Mary's Churchyard, Llanfairpwll.

Miss DAVIES

Miss Cordelia DONNITHORNE (twenty-eight) and/or her sister **Gertrude** (twenty-six) lived at Ivy Cottage with their father. Thomas (sixty-four) government pensioner, and mother, Mary (sixty-four)

Miss FLETCHER

Mrs. FOSTER (Tyn-y-Coed)

Mrs. FRANCIS
Mrs. FURNEAUX
Miss GOODWIN
Mrs. Martha HOLBROOK (forty-five) lived at 3 Alma Terrace with her husband, Thomas (fifty-two) relay clerk, daughters Dorothy Aileen (ten) and Phyllis Mona (eight) and one servant
Miss HOLBROOK probably **Dorothy** and/or **Phyllis**
Mrs. HORRIDGE (Plas Llanfair)
The Misses HUGHES (Llangaffo)
Mrs. HUGHES (Stag Cottage)
**Lady Sarah Elizabeth Hughes-HUNTER
Mrs. JENKINS (Newborough)
Miss Ceri JONES
Miss (Esyllt) **Essie JONES** (Bodlondeb)
Miss Maggie JONES
Mrs. JONES (Bryn Cyrph)
The Misses JONES (Llwyn)
Mrs. JONES (Min-y-Mor)
Mrs. JONES (Snowdon View)
The Misses Morris-JONES
Miss Ceri Parry-JONES (twenty-seven) grocer, owned Maes-y-Don Stores, Llanfaipwll.
Mrs. Jane Ellen MATTHEWS (forty) lived at Liglan Farm with her husband, John (forty-five) veterinary surgeon, daughter Olwen (fourteen) and one servant. Mrs. Matthews died in 1952 and is buried with her husband in St. Mary's Churchyard, Llanfairpwll.
Miss Olwen MATTHEWS (see above – 1911 Census) In WW1 Miss Matthews, then aged about eighteen, was the County Organising Secretary for the Women's War Agricultural Committee. In December 1919 there was a big party for the Anglesey and Caernarfonshire Land Girls before they returned home. Tea was provided, followed by

music and recitations, dancing and games. At that party, the Land Girls presented Miss Matthews with a silver inkwell and photograph frame as a token of their affection, and appreciation of the interest she had always taken in their welfare. She was also the recipient of a beautifully illustrated copy of Charles Dickens' *A Christmas Carol* from the Anglesey and Caernarfonshire Women's War Committee. I think Olwen married Humphrey Griffiths in 1924 – after that I can find no further trace of her.

**Lady Gwen Gertrude NEAVE
**Lady Dorina Lockhart NEAVE
Mrs. OLLOSSON. I originally thought this was Mary, (1901 Census) but on searching the burial records realised it could not have been, as she died in 1907. On the 1911 Census Mary's widower, Samuel (fifty-seven) huntsman, lived at 4 Williams Terrace with sons George (twenty-five) and Charles (eighteen) both employed at the School Slate Works, and daughter Bessie (twenty-one) assistant teacher.

George married Catherine Ellen Jones (twenty-four) on 17 January 1912 at St. Mary's Church, Llanfair Mathafarn Eithaf – so **Mrs. Catherine OLLOSSON** was the WI member. They lived at Minfwrrdd. She died in 1956 and is buried in St. Mary's Churchyard, Llanfairpwll, with her husband.

Miss Eleri OWEN (Garneddwen)
Mrs. Lydia OWEN (twenty-six) lived with her husband, John (thirty-five) schoolmaster, daughters Evelmed (two) and Eleri (born 1901). They employed one servant. Lydia died in 1954 and is buried with her husband in St. Mary's Churchyard, Llanfairpwll.
Mrs. W. OWEN (Menai Bridge)
Mrs. OWEN (Carregddyfnallt)
Mrs. OWEN (Garden Girl-Land Army, Plas Newydd)
Mrs. OWEN (Llandaniel Parsonage)

Mrs. OWEN (The School)

Mrs. PRETTY (FM) I thought she would have been easy to identify but there are three options:

Blanche Mary (sixty-three) who lived with her husband William J. (seventy-five) late coachman, and son George Owen (twenty-six) and grand-daughter Arrianwen (ten) at Salem Terrace, or

Hannah Jane (thirty-three) who lived with her brother William (forty-two) (widower) general contractor, and his daughter Ellen Blanche (thirteen) and son Geraint ap William (eight) at Refail Newydd, or

Mary Ellen (twenty-six) who lived with her husband Hugh (thirty) house painter, daughter Mary Blanche (two) and grand-mother Mary Prichard (seventy) at Fair View Terrace. Mary died in 1953 and is buried in St. Mary's Churchyard, Llanfairpwll.

Miss Blodwen PRICHARD

Miss Ceri PRITCHARD

Mrs. PRITCHARD (Ty Gwyn) (FM)

Mrs. PRYTHERCH (FM)

Mrs. RAINER

Miss RAINEY

Mrs. Bowen-ROBERTS

Mrs. J.O. ROBERTS

Mrs. O. ROBERTS

Mrs. R.W. ROBERTS helped to run the magazine club in 1918

Mrs. ROBERTS (Bodlew, Llandaniel)

Miss ROBERTS (Pwllfanogl)

Mrs. ROBERTS (Tan-y-Coed)

Mrs. ROBERTS (Tyddyn Isa)

Mrs. SARGENT

Mrs. SMITH

Mrs. SOTHEBY (helped the WI but not recorded as a member)

Mrs. **THOMAS** (Bryn Bas)
Mrs. **THOMAS** (Garnedd)
Mrs. **THOMAS** (Pen-y-Bonc) died in 1921
Mrs. **WALKER** (Menai Bridge)
Miss Alice **WILLIAMS**
Miss Gwennie **WILLIAMS**
Mrs. **Ivor WILLIAMS** (Menai Bridge)
Mrs. **J. WILLIAMS**
Miss **K. WILLIAMS**
Miss Mary **WILLIAMS**
Mrs. **T.C. WILLIAMS**
Mrs. **WILLIAMS** (Bryn Goleau)
Mrs. **WILLIAMS** (Min-y-Don) helped to run the magazine club in 1918, librarian 1921.
Miss **WILLIAMS** (Tyn Coed, Llandaniel)
Nurse **WILLIAMS**
Mrs. **WOOLLEY**

Biographies:

Lady **ANGLESEY**, (Victoria) **Marjorie Harriet Paget** (nèe Manners) was born in 1883, the daughter of Henry John Brinsly Manners and (Marion Margaret) Violet, (8th) Duke and Duchess of Rutland. She was a writer and illustrator. She married Charles Alexander Vaughan Paget, the 6th Marquess.

In **1913** Lady Anglesey became the first president of a ladies' society formed to fund the further development of UCNW, which had been founded in 1884.

In **1914** Lady Anglesey attended a Ball at Buckingham Palace. She wore an ivory satin gown embroidered with diamante. Her train, which was attached to her shoulders by large diamond rosettes, was entirely covered in rainbow coloured irridescents. She also wore a diamond tiara and a necklace of three rows of diamonds held together by diamond tassels.

In **August 1916** Lady Anglesey temporarily moved to Ireland because her husband had been appointed military secretary to Sir John Maxwell. As the Easter Rising had taken place only a few months earlier, and Sir John Maxwell had ordered the execution of the leaders, it must have been an extremely dangerous time for an Englishman to be living there, particularly once so closely associated with Sir. John Maxwell.

Victoria's husband was the nephew of Col. Cotton. He allowed the WI to use the Toll Gate House rent-free for more than twenty-five years, donated the plot of land on which their new hall was built, and it was said to be impossible to enumerate his acts of generosity. Whenever the WI was in need, the members never once appealed to him in vain.

Lady Anglesey was known for her generosity with her time, hospitality and money. She was vice-president of the WI and a faithful committee member. During WW2 as well as knitting comforts and learning about first aid and nursing; she marshalled her WI troops into a Women's Home Defence Squad which underwent serious instruction in the use of fire-arms and hand-grenades! Her enthusiasm for this was so great that she presented a challenge cup to be competed for by Llanfairpwll and neighbouring WI's. When Llanfairpwll WI won, she was so excited that she presented the other competitors with prizes as well.

In **1943** Lady Anglesey was Llanfairpwll WI's delegate to the NFWI AGM in London. When Mrs. Davies wrote *A Grain of Mustard Seed* ten years later, she still remembered Lady Anglesey's account – how her word picture brought home to them, the crowds and the excitement. Lady Anglesey had described the steps leading up to the Albert

Hall being all but invisible, covered by women eating their sandwiches; how she had kissed the Queen's hand – accompanying her description with a sweeping curtsey; and how London, for those two days, was made inescapably aware of the WI.

> While she was speaking, we were there – seeing it with her eyes. It was a memorable afternoon.

wrote Mrs. Davies.

Lady Anglesey died in 1933.

Her son, George Charles Henry Victor, 7th Marquess, married **Elizabeth Shirley Vaughan Morgan** who became the National Chairman of the WI.

Mrs. (Rebecca) Bella CLEGG lived at Plas Llanfair with her husband Harry, a solicitor and JP. He was a widower, and with his first wife Sarah, had a son, Rowland, three daughters: Queneida Mary, Edith Winifred and Dorothy Vernon, and almost certainly another son, Humphrey.

Plas Llanfair, home of the Clegg family

Sarah died in July 1884 possibly giving birth to Humphrey. Harry married Bella in October 1885 and they had one son (John) Kay and one daughter, Beatrice Marjorie.

Plas Llanfair was a picturesque mansion on shores of the Menai Strait with extensive grounds, conservatories and ferneries. In 1901 Dorothy (twenty-one), Edith (twenty-two), and Beatrice (nineteen) were still living at home. The Clegg's employed a ladies' maid (who had earlier been the children's nurse) a cook, sewing maid, two house maids, two kitchen maids and a footman.

Sarah had been involved in the life of the village and Bella carried on the tradition. She helped to decorate the church for harvest festivals, attended annual Hunt Balls and provided Christmas treats for the pupils from Llanfairpwll National (Church) School, alternately with Captain and Mrs. Mansell-Morgan.

In **1886** a Primrose Fête and Sports were organised to raise funds for a Primrose Club and Public Newsroom at Menai Bridge. Mrs. Clegg was among the sponsors, being a Dame of the Beaumaris Habitation. The Primrose League

A fête marquee

was set up after Disraeli's death (and named after his favourite flower), to try to popularise Conservatism amongst the working class – the Tories having lost to Gladstone and Liberals in the susbsequent election. All sorts of activities were arranged: high teas, music hall dances, summer fêtes, excursions and cycling clubs to name but a few. Caernarfon-Menai Model Yacht Club organised a Regatta at this fête, Penrhyn Royal Brass Band entertained, and the day was rounded off with sports consisting of all sorts of novelty races e.g. egg and spoon, and sack.

The Anglesey Hunt

The Anglesey Hunt is one of the oldest in Britain. Records show that as early as 1737 there were twenty-five members who paid 5/- each annually; and the total cost of banquets, balls, races and festivities was not to exceed £4-12-6d each year. By 1785 they had a tambourine man to provide the music at the balls at a cost of £5 but paid the poor cook only 5/-! The Hunt Comptroller and Lady Patroness were jointly responsible for organising the week's events.

By 1886, in Hunt Ball season, the Anglesey Harriers met on Tuesday on a local estate and hunted hares. In the evening, the first Ball was held at Beaumaris Town Hall.

Steeplechases took place on Wednesday on the Castle Fields and Fryers Fields at Beaumaris. There was a Ladies' Plate for a prize of the plate and fifty sovereigns, a Farmer's Cup for the cup and twenty sovereigns, the Anglesey Hunt Stakes for ninety sovereigns, The Visitor's Plate for a plate and forty sovereigns, and a Selling Race for twenty-one sovereigns and the chance for the owner to offer the winning horse for sale.

That evening the Ladies' Ordinary was held at the Williams-Bulkeley Arms Hotel, Beaumaris. Usually around 150 ladies and gentlemen attended and were seated in two rooms. (In the very early days the only females present were the wife of the Comptroller and the Lady Patroness). Catering was under the supervision of the Manageress, Miss Williams, and the menu was always in French. The Ball followed.

On Thursday a good day's sport was held on a local estate, after which around fifty huntsmen, their hounds, and fifty carriages (one containing the Cleggs) rode into Beaumaris preceded by the band of the Royal Welch Fusiliers. A large crowd of spectators gathered, awaiting the traditional throwing of hot coppers from the upper windows of the Williams-Bulkeley Arms. This custom is supposed to have originated from the wealthy amusing themselves by throwing heated pennies (with gloved hands) to the poor, and watching them burn themselves! Hopefully, the pennies thrown in Beaumaris were just warmed.

The Gentlemen's Ordinary was held at the hotel that night (this time the menu was in English) and the main Ball followed with dancing until the early hours.

Before Christmas 1886 Mr. and Mrs. Clegg had a huge Christmas Tree delivered to the National School. A sizeable Union Jack was hung across the room to prevent the children seeing the tree and Mrs. Clegg and other ladies decorated it with flags, tapers and prizes. At 3 pm each class was marched out into the playground, the schoolroom was decorated with flags and greenery, and food was laid out. At 3.30 pm 150 children with keen appetites were marched back into the schoolroom and after grace had been said they:

attacked in earnest all the good things set before them.

At 6 pm the Union Jack was removed and the children formed a square around the tree which was lit with a hundred tapers. Mrs. Clegg and the ladies handed a prize, ticketed with the child's name and class to each one. These were:

baskets, carriages, dolls, knives, whips, work-boxes, and other such coveted boyish and girlish property.

As they left with their parents, Mr. and Mrs. Clegg gave each child an orange and sweets.

In **1892** Mr. Harry Clegg was High Sheriff of Anglesey.

The same year, a two-day Bazaar and Fancy Fair was held at Penrhyn Hall, Bangor, to raise funds to extend the hall of residence at UCNW to accommodate fifty students. Penrhyn Hall was decorated to represent Tennyson's *Princesss*, Mrs. and the Misses Clegg manned a stall and the event raised £400.

Mrs. Clegg also supported the RSPCA. At the 1892 AGM at the Queen's Head Café, Bangor, Inspector Yates reported that legal proceedings had been taken in seventy-five cases, mainly horses suffering from chronic and painful disease. Proceedings were taken only in cases of flagrant or persistent abuse or neglect. He was sorry to report that there had been several incidents of rabbit coursing which he been unable to prevent, but it was condemned by all classes. The secretary, Miss Mary Rathbone, then explained that the views of members on vivisection had been canvassed, but there was a divergence of opinion and it was not possible for the society to declare itself either for, or against. However, they felt that the government was not supplying sufficiently detailed information about experiments being carried out on animals, to allow people to reach an informed opinion.

In addition, Mrs. Clegg served on the committee of the Anglesey Working Guild, which had been established in 1887 to look after the poor and sick on the island. At Christmas 1892 the 142 members distributed 300 items including eighty blankets.

In **1894** the first AGM of the Anglesey QM's Needlework Guild was held, Mrs. Clegg was on the

Menai Bridge Lawn Tennis Club, early 1900's

committee. It was decided that clothing and blankets should be distributed only once per year.

Miss Clegg organised a Tennis Tournament in the grounds of Plas Llanfair on behalf of the Society for the Protection of Waifs and Strays, of which she was secretary. It was a fine afternoon and there was an elite crowd to watch the most noted players in the district. Admission was 1/- and tea was served in the conservatory by the Misses Clegg at a cost of 6d. A sum sufficient to maintain one child was raised.

An early photograph of Menai Bridge Brass Band

In **1895** a two day bazaar was organised by Miss Queneida Clegg in aid of the National School, but this was no ordinary bazaar – it had a Parisian stall manned by Henry Cyril Paget, 5th Marquess of Anglesey, who spent a king's ransom on furs, jewels, theatrical costumes and transport! Mrs. and the Misses Dorothy and Edith Clegg had a stall and Messrs Humphrey and Kay Clegg assisted. There were refreshments, and the Menai Bridge Brass Band played musical selections at intervals throughout the two days.

In **1897** Llanfairpwll was decorated with bunting and

the flags of all nations

– to the extent that the houses could hardly be seen!

A greeting arch

There was also an arch and swags of greenery decorated with felicitous mottoes, for the wedding of Mr. Harry Clegg's eldest daughter, such was the respect in which the family and happy couple were held. (On this occasion a special train arrived at the station bringing fifty guests from Liverpool and Chester). The chancel of St. Mary's, Llanfairpwll, was beautifully decorated with towering Palms and Arum Lilies from the conservatories at Plas Llanfair, arranged by the head gardener.

The bride, Queneida, who was given away by her father, wore a dress of rich ivory duchesse satin trimmed with Italian lace, and a satin brocade court train attached to her shoulders with sprays of Orange Blossom. Her tulle veil was secured with a diamond and pearl comb, she also wore a diamond and pearl brooch and carried a bouquet of exotics – all the gifts of the bridegroom, Mr. Stephen Williamson of Neston, Cheshire. (The exotics were possibly Orchids, the first Orchid Society in Britain having been founded in Manchester that year). Her three sisters and cousin were bridesmaids and wore dresses of white spotted silk gauze over green glace silk, trimmed with French Valenciennes lace, and white satin-straw hats trimmed with green and white tulle and pink roses. The service, which was conducted by the Bishop of Bangor and Queneida's brother-in-law-to-be, the Rev. Harry Morgan, was fully choral. As the couple left the church they were cheered by crowds of villagers. The bride's gift to the groom was:

a gun in case

– presumably a gun in **a** case! The staff at Plas Llanfair gave

Plas Llanfair – although taken after the Cleggs had left, this photograph does give an idea of the internal proportions and beautiful windows which looked out onto the Menai Strait

Bollands of Chester

the couple silver dishes and the tenants a magnificent silver epergne all suitably inscribed.

The reception was held in the spacious drawing room and library at Plas Llanfair. Catering, including the wedding cake was by Bollands of Chester. Guests were entertained by music played by a band on the lawn below, drifting through the open windows. Several photographs of the wedding party were taken by J. Wickens of the Retina Studio, Upper Bangor. The happy couple left Bangor by the boat express to sail to Scotland for their honeymoon. In appreciation of all the affection shown by the villagers, Mr. Clegg treated them all – including the children, to a splendid tea. At night there was a firework display and bonfires were lit on surrounding hills.

Subsequent weddings of the Clegg's other daughters followed much the same pattern.

Also in 1897 Mr. and Mrs. Clegg were invited to the Duke and Duchess of Westminster's Summer Ball at Eaton Hall. Many guests drove long distances or opted to stay at

Chester hotels. At Eaton Hall the drives were lit with groups of lamps and stabling had been provided in the park for 200 horses. From 9.30-10 pm a constant stream of carriages arrived in the courtyard. 400 guests were received in the saloon and although the Duke of Westminster was able to remove the sling which he had worn since a recent accident, he had to offer them his left hand to shake.

It was the opinion of the reporter that Eaton Hall never looked better than when it was lit up and that evening it looked superb. He described the saloon with its painted panorama of the Canterbury Pilgrims, and its vaulted ceiling with a golden sun and galaxy of stars on an azure blue background. Both the saloon and the marble hall were decorated with Palms, below which banks of pink and yellow Astilbes, Azaleas, Chrysanthemums, Lilies, Orchids and scarlet Tulips were arranged. The dining-room, where supper was served, contained four long tables and eight smaller ones. Each long table had a Palm as a centerpiece, and each small

Eaton Hall, Chester, home of the Duke and Duchess of Westminster

*Eaton Hall,
the Saloon*

*The Drawing
Room*

The Library

table a silver candelabra, all surrounded by Asparagus ferns and pink and white Begonias. Dancing was in the drawing room where the huge fireplace was filled with Astilbes etc., as was the library – which had become the sitting-out room. Herr Gotlieb's Band (which had recently played for the Royal family at Sandringham), provided the music.

The Duchess of Westminster looked queenly in a dress of pink and silver brocade with a diamond and ruby ornament on the bodice. She also wore a magnificent diamond tiara and diamond serpent necklace.

(Eaton Hall, with the exception of the chapel, clock tower and stable block was demolished in 1961 and replaced by a more modern house).

By **1898** Mrs. Clegg was on the Board of Guardians of the Bangor and Beaumaris Union (Workhouse). A meeting was called to discuss a letter from the local government inspector, questioning whether the doctor should continue in his post, as he had been found on more than one occasion to have neglected inmates. Mrs. Clegg reported that she had visited the institution within the past month and had found the inmates to be clean and comfortable. She had tested the food and found it to be of excellent quality. The board was also informed by the inspector that at the end of the year vaccinations would be discontinued, except where there was reason to fear an outbreak of Smallpox. (No decision was recorded concerning the doctor).

Mrs. Clegg was still serving on the committee of Anglesey QM's Needlework Guild. At the AGM it was resolved:

> that any income this year should be spent, at last, on undergarments for men (as so few were offered to the guild),
> that slightly used clothing would be accepted, and

Staff and Officials, Bangor and Beaumaris Union (Workhouse)

that blankets should be white not coloured.

It was also agreed to hold a show of clothing and blankets at Llangefni.

In **1900** the children from the National School were treated to their annual tea, sports and prize-giving by Mr. and Mrs. Clegg. It was a glorious day and tea was served on long trestle tables on the lawn at Plas Llanfair. Then the children took off – racing down the greensward away from the house towards the Menai Strait. There were both standard and novelty races and the sports were rounded off with a fifteen-minutes each way football match, which resulted in a draw. Giving the children time to catch their breath, a report on the recent scripture exam was read, after which Mrs. Clegg presented the prizes both for the sports and the scripture exam.

The same year Mrs. Clegg sent her apologies for the Anglesey QM's Needlework Guild AGM, at which it was decided that clothing for infants and children up to the age of eight were to be regarded as extras – in addition to the three garments each member agreed to provide each year; and that 200 copies of the rules were to be printed, plus five in Welsh.

In **1901** Mrs. Clegg again sent her apologies for the Anglesey QM's Needlework Guild AGM. Once again some of the decisions were of interest – it was proposed that members who failed to donate three garments could pay a fine of 2/6d instead. After heated discussion this was raised to 5/- but subsequently thrown out, and it was left to local vice-presidents to charge whatever they thought was appropriate. Further animated debate followed about whether white or coloured blankets should be bought and members voted – coloured (blue) blankets won by just two votes. Finally, there was discussion about whether the annual exhibition of clothing and blankets should continue and it was agreed that it should, this year at Baron Hill, Beaumaris.

The same year Caernarfon County School held a Chinese Bazaar at The Pavilion, with the intention of clearing as much as possible of the outstanding £2,000 debt on the school building. This was considered, without doubt, the finest bazaar ever held in the town. Mr. and Mrs. Clegg were patrons. Opening the bazaar, the chairman of the governors stated that they had been criticised on several fronts – some thought that the spectacular location on the Menai Strait and the fine architecture of the school were simply too ambitious, particularly as many children failed to complete their education; but he made no apology for beauty of the site or the building. Further, he could assure patrons that now parents had been convinced of the value of education, very few children dropped out. So far they had achieved three scholarships to Oxford and Cambridge, two to Aberystwyth and ten to UCNW.

The Pavilion had been transformed into a Chinese village with a Pagoda at the centre. The flowers, plants, festoons and Oriental decorations surrounding it were described as:

> most attractive.

Music was provided by the band of the Grenadier Guards. At the entrance to the bazaar a cloakroom had been set up, where it was advertised that patrons could leave everything except children! In fact they could even leave purchases to be parceled up and dispatched to the required addresses. There was a fishpond with a fairy well and magic pump, the purpose was not explained but possibly people were intended to throw in coins. There were several specialist stalls: Advertisements – again unfortunately there is no further information but perhaps the metal ones, Aprons and all manner of household linen – from knitted tea-cosies to exquisite silk and satin eiderdowns, Bric-a-Brac, Chocolates and Sweets, Flowers, Household China, Kitchenalia, Kitchen Store-Cupboard items, Produce – laden with baskets of fruit and vegetables, Toys, and numerous miscellaneous stalls selling everything from pin cushions to massive pieces of carved oak furniture – and on one of these stalls a life-size, china, three-tier wedding cake! There were tea rooms serving hearty savoury pies, dainty cakes, luscious fruit tarts and ice cream, as well as lemonade and tea. And many of the stall holders and ladies serving refreshments were dressed in Oriental costumes.

Entertainment stretched far beyond listening to the band! In the tents outside The Pavilion there were competitions – decorating a ladies' hat for the gentlemen and driving nails into pieces of wood for the ladies. There was also a Ping-Pong Tournament and a Shooting Jungle.

The Phonograph and Cinematograph were demonstrated in one tent, and the brand new wireless telegraphy in another (Marconi having transmitted his first radio signal only four years earlier, in 1897). There were Marionettes and *The Strand-ed Theatre Company* performed humorous sketches and short plays. If all else failed, visitors could retire to the gipsy's tent and have their fortunes told.

Bangor decorated for the Royal Visit

In preparation for the 1902 Royal Visit, Bangor was not satisfied with mere greenery and bunting – houses along the Royal route were freshly painted! In fact

the streets reeked with the smell of wet paint!

The ships in the harbour were flying flags, and Venetian poles hung with flower garlands surrounded the town clock. Long before the expected Royal arrival time, crowds poured into Bangor – many by train, and staked their claim to vantage points. Bethesda quarrymen swelled the ranks having given themselves a holiday – believing that if they worked on Ascension Day, a fatal accident would occur. This superstition was common amongst North Wales quarrymen. HRH Prince George (later King George V) and HRH Princess Mary, the Prince and Princess of Wales, were coming to Bangor to lay the foundation stone for the new wing of the Caernarfonshire and Anglesey Infirmary (which had opened in 1847 at a cost of £1,500). The new wing – containing an operating theatre and board room was going to cost £1,000.

The Royal couple, the Princess wearing a violet dress and toque hat, arrived by Royal train. There were four carriages, two of which had been decorated with the Prince of Wales Plumes and lit by electricity. The mayor and councillors were on the platform to greet the Royal party, which then proceeded by carriage to the Infirmary*. A guard of honour was formed by 200 boys from the bands of the training-ship *Clio* (moored off Bangor) and the Menai Bridge Boy's Brigade. Mr. Harry Clegg, as president of the infirmary and Mrs. Clegg were presented to the Royal couple. The new wing was to be octagonal in shape and joined to the original building by a short corridor. The board room on the ground floor would also be used for Sunday services. The operating theatre on the first floor would be reached by a lift opening into an ante-room. The theatre would have a Terrazzo Mosaic Tile floor, a 5'6" high Sicilian Marble dado, and the top of the walls and ceiling would be treated with Parian Cement, thus enabling the whole area to be washed by hosepipe. A trapped grating into a ventilated down-pipe would allow the water to drain away. There would be both overhead and wall lighting, inlets for ventilation and an electric fan as the means of circulating fresh air and removing exhaust. The architect was Mr. Frank Bellis of Bangor. Mrs. Clegg handed the Prince of Wales a silver trowel and he laid the foundation stone with the words:

I have very great pleasure in laying this foundation stone, and I now declare it well and truly laid!

By the end of the afternoon the new wing was over half-way to being paid for, after sixty school children had presented the Princess with white silk purses containing a minimum of £5 which they had collected. Two purses, presented by a boy and a girl, contained jointly £100 – the gift of the 5th Marquess of Anglesey. The total was £555-13-9d. The purses were returned to the children as keepsakes of the occasion. Their Royal Highnesses inspected two wards before leaving.

*Remarkable film of the procession can be seen on-line at: https://player.bfi.org.uk>free>film>watch-royal-visit-to-bangor-1902-1

They were then driven by carriage to the Faenol Estate, where they were to be guests of Mr. and Mrs. Assheton-Smith. Along the route they passed several miles of flags, bunting, and streamers and a magnificent greenery arch with the greeting:

Ever Welcome.

Outside Faenol Grand Lodge a massive dome of streamers had been constructed, and a great crowd of estate workers, tenants, and visitors from Port Dinorwig (Y Felinheli) and Caernarfon had gathered to welcome the Royal couple. As soon as they were recognised a huge cheer went up, which the Prince and Princess acknowledged.

In **1907** Mrs. Clegg attended a garden party in aid of the Society for the Protection of Waifs and Strays held at Faenol, Port Dinorwig, the home of Mrs. Assheton-Smith*.

Canon Fairchild explained that the society had started off in St. Asaph twenty-five years ago with donations of thirteen postage stamps and last year alone they had collected £100,000. There were five homes in North Wales, four of them in the Bangor diocese, including Arthog (boys) at Harlech, St. Mark's (boys) at Caernarfon, and Tregarth (girls). Unfortunately the society was £500 in debt, but this certainly was not due to a lack of sympathy on the part of local residents – rather to the expansion of their work. The secretary of the society, Rev. E. de M. Rudolph then said that he was proud that no member of the clergy would ever come across a destitute child and be unable to give them a home. He added that he personally was particularly interested in the homes for cripples, where, like the able-bodied, older children were taught skills which would enable them to earn their own livings. So successful was this venture, that the demand to employ these young adults outstripped the supply.

Everyone then trooped indoors to the ballroom where they were entertained by a production of *Pierrot of the Minute*. Mademoiselle Marguerite 'Rita' Lucille Jolivot** played the Moon Maiden with:

> exquisite charm and demonstrating the possession of remarkable histrionic powers.

So many people wanted to see the show that there had to be two performances. Tea was provided, and afterwards visitors could stroll in the grounds, and listen to Llanrug Brass Band. Later Mdlle Jolivot donned a Welsh costume and danced on the lawn outside the mansion.

*Mrs. Assheton-Smith was the widow of George William Duff Assheton-Smith, who inherited the Faenol estate from his great uncle, Thomas Assheton-Smith (who had been

178

vehemently opposed to the building of the Menai Bridge, refused to use it, and chose to continue to cross the Strait by boat for the rest of his life!). On his marriage in 1888, George returned half of their rents for that year to his tenants by way of celebration. A devoted royalist, for HM Queen Victoria's Diamond Jubilee, he paid for all his workers and their wives to travel by train to London and stay for four days. He also gave each worker half-a-crown spending money. Meanwhile, back at home, George had a hill on his estate planted with trees and shrubs to form: JUBILEE GWDAS (his initials) 1897.

As well as bison roaming in the park, he had an exotic zoo! By the time he died in 1904, the estate covered 36,000 acres and supported 1,600 tenants. He had often commented that he could walk the fifteen miles from Faenol to the summit of Snowdon, without ever once stepping off his land.

**Mdlle. Jolivot was already a well known actress by the time she appeared at Faenol. Later she was one of the survivors of the Lusitania, sunk by a German u-boat in WW1.

In **1909** Mr. Harry Clegg died at home, Plas Llanfair, at the age of sixty-six. He had double pneumonia but seemed to be making good progress and had been pronounced out of danger, when he suffered a sudden relapse. After a short service at his home, Mr. Clegg's coffin – which could not even be glimpsed due to the number of beautiful floral tributes covering it, was conveyed to St. Mary's Church, Llanfairpwll. It was watched over throughout the night by relays of his tenants. The following day his funeral service was conducted by the Bishop of Bangor and he was laid to rest in the family vault with his first wife, Sarah. It is worth noting that at the time of Harry's death, his eldest son, Rowland, spoke of Bella as his mother – not his step-mother, and said that she treated both Sarah's children and her own equally. During WW1 Mrs. Clegg was commandant of Bodlondeb Red Cross Military Hospital, Bangor. After the war she joined the RSPCA Executive Committee and was appointed as a special badge member. This meant she would be recognised in her official capacity by anyone she challenged concerning cruelty to an animal, whilst still reporting more serious cases to the Inspector.

In **1917** Mrs. Clegg attended a sale in aid of Bodlondeb Military, and Penrhyn Cottage Red Cross Hospitals. It was held in business premises opposite Bangor Market Hall and the interior could easily have been mistaken for an art gallery that day. Prospective bidders were entertained by Mrs. Gough's Orchestra. The sale was opened by Mrs. Lloyd George and included 3,000 cartoons of notable people (many of them autographed), which had been published in *Vanity Fair*. There were several of Mr. Lloyd-George and prospective buyers were assured that he would autograph them.

In the middle of all the art and jewellery a

Jerusalem pony

was put up for sale – this turned out to be a donkey described as:

sound of wind and limb

and allegedly brought back from Palestine by General Allenby, presented to HM King George V, and donated by the King to the Red Cross. The creature was sold to the Rev C. Barlow of Bangor for £5.

In recognition of her war work, Mrs. Clegg was invited by HM King George V and HM Queen Mary to a garden party at Buckingham Palace and at some point she was also awarded the MBE. After the war, due to Mrs. Clegg's generosity, a new social club was established in Menai Bridge which was so well supported it soon needed an extension!

Mrs. Clegg died in **1937** at the age of ninety. Her obituary said:

> She was generous to the poor and needy and a supporter of every good cause. She will be sadly missed by many to whose homes she brought sunshine and happiness.

She was buried with her husband in St. Mary's Churchyard, Llanfairpwll.

Col. Hon. Richard Southwell George Stapleton-COTTON was born in 1848 in Lancashire, the second son of the second Viscount Combermere of Bhurtpore who was killed in a horse and carriage accident. He became famous

for the fact that, on the day of his funeral, a photograph taken in the empty library of his home (Combermere Abbey) when developed, appeared to show a shadowy man sitting in his favourite armchair!

The Stapleton-Cottons had been wealthy – as well as Combermere Abbey in Lancashire, they owned extensive estates in the West Indies, but Col. Cotton's father had lost a lot of money in India.

In 1870 Col. Cotton

Col. the Hon. Richard Stapleton-Cotton with Tinker

married the Hon. Jane Charlotte Methuen. In 1879 he fought in the Zulu War, during which his tent was struck by lightning and his legs were paralysed from the knees down. From 1889-91 he was Inspector General of Police in British Guiana. About **1900** he arrived at Plas Llwynonn: on the estate of his nephew, the 5th Marquess of Anglesey. He and his wife lived there and employed a cook, parlour maid, two house maids, kitchen maid and a coachman.

Col. Cotton industriously set up a bacon factory, an egg collection depot, and bulb and chicory farms. He also grew onions and tobacco. The egg collection depot is particularly worthy of mention. Col. Cotton introduced the grading of eggs and paid commission on eggs received at the depot. He provided two Ford vans for the collection of eggs and London and North Western Railways (LNWR) built a large warehouse actually on Llanfairpwll Station to aid the eggs onward transmission. In the second year he sold nearly one and a half million eggs and added £500 to LNWR's income

Newborough rush-mat makers with Col. the Hon. Stapleton-Cotton

– for carriage, in addition to the rent he paid for the use of the warehouse.

In **1907** Col. Cotton organised an exhibition and sale on behalf of the Anglesey Industries Association at Parciau, Moelfre. Anglesey Industries promoted not only large concerns, but true cottage industries – helping them to improve quality and find markets for their goods. They also tried to ensure that local arts and crafts did not die out. Basket-makers, knitters, leather-workers, metal-workers, weavers and wood-carvers were all represented. Col. Cotton also took a great interest in rush-mat making from local Maram Grass at Newborough.

Towards the end of 1907 it was noted in the *Chester Courant* that Col. Cotton had recently published a book entitled: *Cottage Gardens – practical hints on cultivation and management*, which it claimed, was mainly for the working classes. In the preface the Duchess of Sutherland wrote that:

It is especially valuable for the fact that it can be studied and understood by all: and its precepts followed equally by those with book-learning and those without.

The reviewer commented:

Open the book at any page and the minutest directions will be found, invaluable to any man handling a spade and setting to work to make his garden profitable. No cottager could be mystified, nothing is left to chance, no instruction can bear two meanings, what a man should do and avoid is imparted in language as clear as daylight and most unmistakeable plainness.

He continued that few gentlemen had done as much for their poorer neighbours as Col. Cotton, and that any profits from the sale of the book would be used to set up a scholarship for the sons of agricultural-labourers or other working men in receipt of ordinary wages, at Harper-Adams Agricultural College, Staffordshire. The small volume became extremely popular and there was a second edition in 1909. Col. Cotton also translated a booklet: *Economical Dinners for Workers* into Welsh and this sold for 1d.

In **1908** homespuns, needlework, dairy, and farm and garden produce had been added to the items on sale at the Anglesey Industries event, held this year at Penrhos, Holyhead, and Col. Cotton had also engaged the Holyhead Orchestral Band. In addition there were a lot of musical competitions for: boys and girls solos, boys and girls action songs, soprano, contralto, tenor and baritone solos; and glee clubs.

This appears to have become an annual event and by **1909** had moved to Baron Hill, Beaumaris and expanded to include not only the Anglesey Industries exhibitors but what would now be advertised as a fun day out for all the family! Present were: Beaumaris Musical Entertainers, Llanfairpwll Prize Choir, Menai Bridge Brass Band, the Penllinon Singers, Telynor Gwalia, a gramophone under the direction of Mr. W.H. Morgan, a coconut shy and miniature rifle range, tea and refreshments. Once again the organiser was Col. Cotton, who was of the opinion that the greater the crowd he could attract, the better the prospects for the craftsmen of selling their products.

Col. Cotton's bulb fields were packed with Daffodils, Hyacinths and Tulips and must have looked beautiful before the flowers were cut, packed into boxes and despatched from the station. In 1909 it was reported that in 1907 7,000 bulbs had been planted as an experiment, in 1908 100,000 and by 1909 the number had increased to 400,000. Col. Cotton thought that bulb growing was unlikely to be profitable for anyone attempting to do it on a small scale, but done on a large scale would yield good returns. He added that the Anglesey bulbs had been examined by an expert and were deemed to be of very high quality.

In **1913** Col. Cotton also used a quarter of an acre of rich loam to grow tobacco, which resulted in a crop claimed to be as good as any in Britain.

In **1915** Col. Cotton was appointed to a committee to recruit women to work on the land in Anglesey. They were given the option of milking, thinning turnips or other seedlings, harvesting or general farm work.

Col. Cotton also supplied 100 blackcurrant and 200 gooseberry bushes, as well as 500 raspberry canes to local schools, to encourage children to take up gardening.

The same year, when Anglesey's dairy farmers were getting only 10d. per pound for their butter, which was then sold on at 1/3d per pound, Col. Cotton advised the farmers to turn their milk into cheese instead, for which there would be a much greater demand. And when someone else at the meeting suggested introducing dairy produce auctions similar to those held in Dorset, Col. Cotton offered to pay the rail fares for two dairymen to travel to Dorset to see how the auctions were organised.

Also in 1915 Col. Cotton spoke out forcefully about two problems which beset local farmers and gardeners – namely the poor quality of seeds and fertilisers available to them. He urged them to read a leaflet on the subject produced by UCNW and obtainable in English or Welsh, free of charge.

In **1916** Col. Cotton, through the AOS, took a great interest in a fruit and vegetable growing scheme: Agricultural Produce Supplies Ltd. which had been set up at Kinmel Camp by the military. The object was to source fresh food locally. When the 68th (Welsh) Division was stationed at Bedford, Colonel Frewen was highly dissatisfied with the supply and quality of food provided for his regiment. A conference was arranged to discuss this, and the Commanding Officer of another regiment, Captain E.S. Williams-Ellis, whose home was in North Wales, mentioned the Criccieth WI Market organised by Mrs. Drage. He

Entrance to Kinmel Military Camp

suggested that it would be a good idea to contact the AOS which was closely involved with the Criccieth venture. Col. Frewen arranged to meet Mr. Nugent-Harris (AOS) and the operation at Kinmel Camp was set up. As much fruit and as many vegetables as possible were bought locally, but because initially local growers could not meet the demand, extra supplies were brought from Liverpool by rail. They earnestly hoped that in due course all produce would be supplied by local farmers, market gardeners and even individual allotment and garden owners. A huge corrugated-iron shed had been erected at the entrance to the camp and there all the produce was sorted (in military fashion!), and whatever was not required for feeding the soldiers at Kinmel Camp was sold. Local growers were assured of a fair price for their produce and any small profit went directly to the War Office. In time the scheme was widened to include other foodstuffs. This necessitated a central depot in London and it was established close to the Army and Navy Stores. It was first known as the Army Canteen Board, and became the Navy, Army and Air Force Institute: the NAAFI – and all thanks to Mrs. Drage and Criccieth WI!

The same year, 1916, together with the 6th Marquess of Anglesey, Col. Cotton set up a two year scheme to teach women gardening with a view to them obtaining work as gardeners, or as forewomen in larger gardens where teams of gardeners were employed. Practical work would be carried out in the gardens of both the Marquess and Col. Cotton, which jointly covered several acres. Students would gain experience in growing fruit and vegetables, glasshouse crops and in vineries. Theoretical work would be undertaken at UCNW in the autumn and winter months. Preference would be given to Welsh speaking applicants from Anglesey, but after that, the course would be extended to Caernarfonshire and the rest of Wales if necessary. Students would receive payment more than sufficient to cover their board and lodgings. It was hoped that grants to cover expenses incurred by attending classes at the university could be arranged.

In **1917**, long before the government realised there would be food shortages, there was a campaign on Anglesey to encourage people to have allotments. However, this had not taken off until Col. Cotton got involved and rapid progress was then made. Farmers helped initially by ploughing the land. Col. Cotton bought sufficient seed potatoes for all allotment owners and allowed them to pay by instalments. It was his intention to provide fertiliser in the same way at the end of the season, also to provide monetary prizes for the best cropped allotments. It was noted that as sugar was not available for jam-making, some sugar-beet would be grown which could be used with less acidic fruit, and vegetable marrows. Col. Cotton also grew onions: which were supposed to be impossible to grow in Wales. He recounted how he used to see the French Onion-men selling their wares and wondered if it would be possible to grow them? He started off in a very small way and by 1918 was using two acres. He estimated that it cost him £100 an acre to grow them and they would yield in excess of ten tons per acre. A few weeks earlier French onions had been fetching £65 per ton, so he would certainly make a good profit.

In **1918** Col. Cotton opened the second Bangor Annual Horticultural Show, which was held at Penrhyn Hall and attracted a large crowd. The Mayor reported that there were 300 allotments in Bangor and he hoped they would continue after the war ended. He had every reason to believe that they would – given the enthusiasm of the holders. This show was in its infancy, but he hoped that next year there would also be exhibits from the gardeners at the great houses in the locality – which would set the standard for allotment holders to aim for. The Mayor also paid tribute to Col. Cotton, saying how fortunate they were to have such a passionate and experienced gardener in their midst.

Col. Cotton congratulated the allotment holders on their zeal and the magnificent quality of their crops. He added that he was so impressed he would present a cup the following year. He also stressed the importance of being able to sell surplus produce and promised that a scheme would be in place throughout Caernarfonshire by the following season.

In **1919** Col. Cotton presided at the AGM of the North

Wales branch of the Welsh National Association for Reconstruction (after WW1). Miss Mary Rathbone was secretary and outlined what the branch had looked at in its first year – agriculture: particularly wages, conditions and the resettlement of ex-servicemen, social life in the villages and the necessity of having a meeting hall in each community, and water. The purpose of this meeting was mainly to consider the supply of water and electricity. Two streams had been identified as suitable, but the effect their development for power generation would have on the life and industry of the villages on their banks, needed to be carefully considered. Also transport was poor and they intended to try to find out whether an electric railway would be viable. A resolution was passed to urge the Board of Trade Water Power Resources Committee to carry out an urgent survey in North Wales. (I was shocked to learn that even in the early 1920s, Llanfairpwll had neither running water nor electricity).

The same year Col. Cotton must have been delighted as president, to open a Horticultural Show for allotment holders and gardeners at the Council School in his home village. Miss Watts (Aberbraint) from the WI was one of the judges of the Llanfairpwll Show.

Col. Cotton took great interest in the Anglesey Farmer's Co-operative Society, served on military tribunals, was a member of UCNW Council, and in 1919 was appointed deputy-lieutenant of Anglesey. Like the Suffragettes,

Deeds not Words

was his motto! It is easy to forget that all this was achieved whilst being confined to a wheelchair. Col. Cotton's love of colour extended to his knitting, he turned all his wife's odds and ends of wool into brightly patterned garments. One lady commented that if he would knit one for her she would wear it for gardening, and should anyone she did not wish to see arrive, she would throw herself into a flower-bed and thus render herself undetectable! He did knit one for her and when the jumper was admired by HRH Princess Victoria on a visit to Bodlondeb Military Hospital, Col. Cotton knitted one for her too.

The Hon. Mrs. Jane Stapleton-Cotton

He married **Jane Charlotte**, daughter of Frederick, 2nd Baron Methuen and Anna Horatia Caroline. The Stapleton-Cotton's had six children, two of whom pre-deceased them.

As we know, Mrs. Cotton was the beloved president of Llanfairpwll WI from its inception until her death in 1924. She was described as:

unostentatious, hospitable, gracious and, like her husband, always helping others.

In **1902** Mrs. Cotton attended a reception at Buckingham Palace. She wore a gown of white and gold spangled tissue (which was a very lustrous and softly draping fabric) with flounces of beautiful, old Venetian lace, and a train of cream brocade lined with satin.

In **1908** Col. and Mrs. Cotton sailed to the West Indies and in **1910** they and eight other guests sailed on the 6th

Marquess of Anglesey's yacht, Semiramis, to Gibraltar.

During WW1 Mrs. Cotton was chairman of both the Land Girls and Women's War Agricultural Committees for Anglesey and Caernarfonshire. As early as **1914** Belgian refugees were accommodated at Plas Newydd, the home of the 6th Marquess and Lady Anglesey and Mrs. Cotton was very kind to the women and children – organising entertainment for them whenever she could.

When Mrs. Cotton died in **1924** she was deeply mourned by all who knew her – particularly by members of the WI. After his wife's death, Col Cotton had one of his legs amputated, but had already decided to return to the West Indies, specifically to St. John's, Antigua, where he still owned a cotton plantation. Despite his recent operation he set off on his voyage with cheerfulness and optimism, and in a letter to a friend, mentioned that for the first time in twenty years he was free from physical pain. As a mark of their affection and esteem his friends in North Wales subscribed to give him a parting gift:

> We cannot let you pass from our midst without some tangible expression of our personal affection and of our admiration for your devoted and untiring work for our community.

The gift was a motor car, but before it could be despatched, Col. Cotton died of Dysentery.

Mrs. Davies, author of *A Grain of Mustard Seed* regarded him as:

> (the WI's) founder, guide, and helper, it's inspiration and its architect ... to him the members looked for spiritual direction, for business advice and for practical assistance. Whenever they were in doubt, the committee sent a deputation to Col. Cotton.

Within twenty years of Col. Cotton's death, a WI had been established within a few miles of the plantation he owned. The president of Sandy Point WI, St. Kitts, Leeward Islands, Miss Wilhelmina Armatrading wrote to the WI members at Llanfairpwll that she had returned home to St. Kitts from America the day after Col. Cotton died. Straight away she connected his name to the Stapleton Estate, and on enquiring, found that she was correct. She said it was:

> a beautiful estate on a hill in St. Peter's Parish, commanding a fine view of the sea ...
>
> many persons remember his visits and the difficulty in getting him from the ship, his being taken about in a wheelchair; also his acts of benevolence and consideration for his employees. He certainly was a fine personality from all I have heard. He would be happy to know that WI's have reached St. Kitts and, would you believe it, we are jealous that he died on Antigua instead of here. I was sorry when I found that out. We would have taken pleasure in beautifying his grave with flowers.

Tinker Stapleton-COTTON, the Colonel's beloved little dog, went everywhere with him and was a paid-up member of Llanfairpwll WI.

Mrs. Mansell-MORGAN (Plas Coed Mor) The National School's children's Christmas treat was provided alternately by Mr. and Mrs. Clegg and Captain and Mrs. Mansell-Morgan. In **1892** it was the turn of the latter. This year there were races with prizes from Capt. Mansell-Morgan, and after tea each child received a bun, a bag of sweets and a toy. Capt. Mansell-Morgan also provided a good Christmas meal and entertainment by choirs for the older residents of Llanfairpwll.

In **1896** Capt. and Mrs. Mansell-Morgan's daughter, Lillie, married Mr. Harry Duff JP. (the brother of Mr. George William Duff Assheton-Smith who inherited the Faenol Estate). It can probably be described as:

the wedding of the year!

The ceremony, which was fully choral, took place at the beautifully decorated Llandysilio Church, conducted by the Bishop of Bangor. The bride, who was given away by her father, wore a dress of richest ivory duchesse satin, covered with old Brussels lace from her mother's wedding gown. The bodice was draped with chiffon, and trimmed with lace and Orange Blossom; and a long court train was attached to the shoulders. She wore a small coronet of Orange Blossom and a tulle veil fixed with three diamond stars, the gift of the bridegroom. She carried a magnificent bouquet, also the gift of the groom. Lillie had eight bridesmaids, the chief being her sister. They wore white satin dresses, the bodices lightly draped with chiffon, with yellow velvet at the neck and waist, and white felt hats trimmed with yellow velvet and white ostrich feathers. They also wore pearl brooches formed into the initials of the bride and groom – gifts of the groom, and carried bunches of Lilies of the Valley in honour of the bride. Mrs. Mansell-Morgan wore a dress of dark ruby velvet, with Brussels lace over a salmon satin bodice. She also wore a ruby velvet cape with a sable collar and matching toque hat.

The groom's gifts to the bride were a diamond half hoop ring, a pearl half hoop ring, a diamond and pearl keeper ring, a diamond pin, two diamond bracelets – one with her initial and the other with a horseshoe, and three diamonds mounted as a tiara. In addition, the bride received fifteen other pieces of diamond jewellery from wedding guests. The staff at Plas Coed Mor (the bride's home) gave the couple a wrought iron standard lamp. The indoor servants at Faenol (the groom's home) gave them a silver tea service, and the outdoor staff, a silver coffee pot. The workmen on the Faenol Estate gave silver spoons and a silver crumb scoop and the quarrymen at Port Dinorwig, silver candlesticks. The children of the National School gave them a photograph album and two of the more unusual gifts were a bottle of gulf seaweed and a goldfinch in a gilt cage.

The reception, for several hundred people was held at the George Hotel, Bangor Ferry. The weather was perfect. Menai Bridge and Port Dinorwig (homes of the bride and groom respectively) and even Bangor and Caernarfon were swathed in bunting and from the steamship *Vaynol*, moored in the river opposite the George Hotel, guns salutes were periodically fired. The couple left Bangor by train for Chester and onwards to the continent for their honeymoon. Lillie's going away outfit sounds truly spectacular – a grey dress trimmed with grey velvet and silver passementerie (metallic lace); a pink velvet waistcoat overlaid with white spotted gauze; a pink velvet cape lined with pink silk and with a grey fox fur collar; and a grey velvet toque hat trimmed with pink roses and white osprey feathers.

Afterwards, tea was given to the school children in Port Dinorwig, and the foresters on the Faenol estate were treated to a sumptuous meal. At night the houses and shops at Port Dinorwig were illuminated with Chinese lanterns and several bonfires were lit – including a massive one on the Faenol Estate which could be seen for miles around. There were also fireworks. And the school children's teas, fireworks and bonfires were repeated in both Menai Bridge and Llanfairpwll!

In **1900** Captain Mansell-Morgan died. In the **1911** Census Mrs. Mansell-Morgan was fifty-six and still living at

Plas Coed Mor, with her son (twenty-seven), and a butler, cook, housemaid and kitchen maid.

Mrs. Mansell-Morgan was on the WI committee and became president immediately after Mrs. Cotton's death, until ill health forced her to resign in November 1926. She was also a Dame of the Menai Bridge Habitation of the Primrose League.

John Stanley's Butcher's Shop, Beaumaris – which advertised that their meat came from animals slaughtered by Lady Hughes-Hunter's humane killer

Lady Sarah Elizabeth Hughes-HUNTER, (Plas Coch) was Lady of the Manor of Cemaes, Anglesey.

A cause close to her heart was coastal erosion and in **1907** she applied to the Board of Trade to issue an order banning the carting away of sand and shingle from the beach at Cemaes Bay.

In **1908** Lady Hughes-Hunter was reported to have been taking an active interest in the more humane killing of animals and was promoting a series of petitions to parliament to try to amend current practice. At the **1909** RSPCA AGM it was reported that she had donated two humane killers for the use of Anglesey butchers. The same year, a petition containing over one thousand signatures started by Lady Hughes-Hunter, which requested that cattle should be killed by an instantaneous method, was presented to parliament. Also in 1908 Lady Hughes-Hunter attended a garden party at Plas Coch, Penmaenmawr, in aid of the Band of Mercy. This was an offshoot of the RSPCA intended to teach children to be kind to animals. By 1909 about 500 Bands of Mercy had been established in schools and Sunday Schools, and the children met fortnightly or monthly for lectures – particularly on how to look after their pets. Inspector Reeks from the RSPCA said he was of the opinion that in the majority of cases people were not deliberately cruel – but were thoughtlessly cruel, and education could certainly improve the lives of domestic animals. Lady Hughes-Hunter then presented prizes to children from Penmaenmawr National School's Band of Mercy, who had won a competition for the best drawings and essays on kindness to animals.

In **1910** Lady Hughes-Hunter presented her daughter, (Ethel) Marjory, at Court at Buckingham Palace. Marjorie wore a white satin gown trimmed with sparkling chiffon, bugle beads and pearls, and a pearl necklace.

In the **1911** Census residents at Plas Coch were: William Bulkeley Hughes-Hunter (thirty) son, Elizabeth (thirty-three) daughter, Anne (twenty-six) daughter, together with a retired butler, his daughter who was the cook, and three housemaids.

The fact that Lady Hughes-Hunter took herself off to London every winter, renting houses in such fashionable areas as Eaton Square (built by the Duke of Westminster and named after Eaton Hall, Chester), and remained there until spring, may explain why she was absent for the Census.

In **1914** Lady Hughes-Hunter presented her daughter, Mrs. Gerald White, at Court at Buckingham Palace on the occasion of her marriage. The new bride wore an ivory satin robe with flounces of Point D'Alcenon lace (from Northern France), with an ivory brocade cape, patterned with roses and lined with chiffon. She wore ornaments of diamonds and pearls.

The same year, Lady Hughes-Hunter was able to secure Dr. Charles Reinhardt, chairman of the Council of Justice for Animals, to speak at a public meeting in Bangor, about the desirability of having a public abattoir in the town. In the event he was unable to attend but was replaced by Captain Turner from the RSPCA. There were at that time, ten private abattoirs in Bangor and it was impossible for these to be properly inspected. With one public abattoir the treatment of the animals, hygiene, and carcasses could be constantly inspected by a qualified veterinary surgeon, able to detect even the smallest amount of disease and prevent infected meat from reaching the butcher's shops. At the end of the meeting the proposition for a public abattoir was put to the vote, but the result was equally divided for and against.

Like Col. Cotton, Lady Hughes-Hunter was a supporter of Anglesey Industries. As a result of the work of the Anglesey QM's Needlework Guild, of which she was also a member, at Christmas 1914 the soldiers of the 2nd Battalion Royal Welch Fusiliers who were guarding the bridges and cables at Menai Bridge, Conway and Abergeirch, received handsome presents comprising: a shirt, a pair of socks, a Welsh Testament, a pipe, tobacco and cigarettes, shaving soap, two handkerchiefs, chocolate and a greetings card. In addition, Miss Davies of Menai Bridge gave the servicemen tickets for the Cinematograph Palace on Christmas Day and Boxing Day, and tea and entertainment on New Year's Eve and New Year's Day.

In **1915** Lady Hughes-Hunter became a patron of the North Wales Nursing Association which was desperately in need of funds. Apart from annual donations of at least £10, patrons contributed their signatures to a list which was lithographed and sold to autograph collectors.

At Christmas the same year Lady Hughes-Hunter was amongst those helping to make it a happy time for patients and staff at the Penhesgyn Open-Air Children's Convalescent Home in Menai Bridge. In the afternoon they were entertained by a conjuror and a ventriloquist, then after singing carols were given presents.

In **1919** she joined the RSPCA Executive Committee and, like Mrs. Clegg, was appointed a special badge member: enabling her to officially challenge anyone she suspected of cruelty.

Note: Lady Gwen Neave died only a year after Llanfairpwll WI was formed so her association was brief, but she is included because her engagements give an insight into life in a different and more industrial part of the island.

Subsequently, her daughter-in-law, Lady Dorina Neave, had connections with the WI in Anglesey.

Lady Gwen Gertrude NEAVE (Llys Dulas)

In **1872** there was great rejoicing when Sir Arundel, 4th Baronet, and Lady Gwen Neave returned to Llys Dulas from their honeymoon in Italy. She was the daughter of the 1st Baron Dinorben of Kinmel Park, who also had a house at Amlwch. Both Lady Gwen and her mother, Lady Dinorben, were already household names in the locality for their concern with, and kindness to, the poor. It had been

Llys Dulas, home of the Neave family

intended to organise a celebration when Sir Arundel and Lady Gwen were married the previous autumn, but the bride preferred to wait until they returned home. So the Welcome Home Committee had organised a luncheon at the Dinorben Arms, the distribution of 200 packets of tea to elderly women, and oranges, buns and pennies to 1,200 school children.

When Sir Arundel and Lady Gwen arrived at Amlwch Station it was gay with flowers, greenery, flags, and a triumphal arch, and red carpet had been laid to the waiting carriage. Sir Arundel was immediately congratulated on his choice as his partner in life:

> a lady who by her amiability, goodness of heart, affable condescension to all around her, and her overflowing unostentatious deeds of charity to the poor, has endeared her to all who have had the pleasure of her acquaintance.

Llanerchymedd String Band played as the couple made their way to the brougham. They were driven around the town to see all the decorations – Amlwch being portrayed as a massive flower garden interspersed with flags of every colour. As well as the usual arches and mottoes, various people had taken to painting pictures depicting Lady Gwen's kindness:

> annual overcoats for miners and clothing for the needy; weekly provisions and a wagon of coal at Christmas; fountains for the thirsty; educating children and visiting the sick.

and poetry:

> Old Mona waking to receive
> Sir A brave and Lady Neave.
> Our hearts with thousand welcomes burn
> We bless the day of their return.
> And fervent prayers ascend above
> For blessings on their blended love.
> Upon their race may heaven smile
> While waters clasp old Mona's Isle.

The Pork Shop had evergreens, flags and a fully grown, decorated sheep (not pig!) on the roof. The gift of a silver salver from the inhabitants of Amlwch was placed at the head of the table in the artistically and tastefully decorated pavilion, at the rear of the Dinorben Arms. Luncheon, at 2.30 pm was considered sumptuous and served with the elegance and style for which this hostelry had long been famed. Llannerchymedd String Band played again in the interval between the meal and the numerous toasts, and the proceedings continued until a late hour. In the late afternoon 950 school and Sunday School children marched through the village singing in both Welsh and English, the words specially penned to fit the occasion. At 10 pm a balloon was sent up followed by fireworks, and bonfires blazed on surrounding heights.

After the celebration organised for them by Amlwch and Pensarn Committees, Sir Arundel and Lady Gwen demonstrated their gratitude by hosting a series of events starting the following Monday with a party at Llys Dulas for personal friends. This was followed on Tuesday by a dinner for the thirty men who comprised the Amlwch Committee, the only ladies present being Lady Gwen and Mrs. Captain Henry Mitchell, wife of the committee chairman. The long table was elegantly decorated with flowers, mosses and ferns, the centre-piece being a beautiful silver epergne – the wedding gift of the Amlwch Committee. The evening light was excluded and the spacious dining room was lit exclusively by candelabra and candles, arranged down the whole length of the table and sideboard. Other wedding presents were also displayed, including another graceful epergne – the gift of the Pensarn Committee and gifts from the farm labourers and school children. The dinner was described as exquisite – and the service incomparable.

Guests took tea and coffee in the drawing room before leaving at about 11 pm. The dinner on Wednesday was for the gentlemen of the Pensarn Committee, who were treated with the same courtesy and kindness and, as many of them were English, they were assured that they should feel free to converse in their own language. On Thursday evening the tenants and their families, numbering over 160, were entertained to dinner in the great hall. This time there were five long tables – decorated as beautifully as on earlier occasions, and the meal was considered superb. And on Friday it was the turn of the farm servants and their families to be treated to dinner. On each occasion Sir Arundel sat at the head of the table and Lady Gwen opposite him at the other end. It was said that it was difficult to know who was more delighted with the parties – the host and hostess or their numerous guests. On Saturday 100 school children sat down in the great hall to a roast beef dinner followed by plum pudding.

An article in the *The North Wales Chronicle* gave an insight into how the Neaves spent a typical week when they were on Anglesey. They left Dagnam Park in Essex early on Monday, arriving at Llys Dulas in the evening. They spent Tuesday visiting their elderly pensioners and the poor of the neighbourhood, taking care to visit first the sickest and most needy. On Wednesday they entertained a shooting party at which masses of pheasants, woodcock and hares were bagged. Thursday they spent at the Cottage Hospital visiting the patients and regularly inspected the building and furnishings – if any repairs or improvements were required, Sir Arundel covered the cost. On Friday Lady Gwen distributed clothing to poor children (particularly knitted items and warm under-clothing) through the Dorcas Society and on Saturday soup was distributed in vast quantities from Llys Dulas – Sir Arundel having supervised its preparation!

Also in 1872, there was a great scandal when Rev. Hugh Owen, Rector of Llanerchymedd was charged with:

at divers [*sic*] times during the past two years being in a state of intoxication, particularly at a lunch at the Dinorben Arms, Amlwch, to celebrate the return of Sir Arundel and Lady Gwen to Llys Dulas.

No result was recorded!

In **1875** Lady Gwen donated monetary prizes for a

ploughing match held at Plas Uchaf Farm, Llanwenllwyfo. Twenty teams took part and were required to plough furrows six inches deep and five inches wide, over an area of an acre. Dinner was provided by Mr. Elias, the owner of the farm.

The same year, in their absence, Sir Arundel and Lady Gwen arranged for blankets, counterpanes, shirts, overcoats, petticoats and shawls to be distributed to 250 of the poor and needy. This was an annual event which took place just before Christmas. In subsequent years, when Lady Gwen could attend, she personally helped the recipients to find their correct sizes and try them on, which was thought to be very arduous for her! She also paid for thirty 1/- loaves to be distributed each day for the coming three months.

In **1876** New Year was celebrated at Llys Dulas with unusual festivities, this being the first time Sir Arundel and Lady Gwen had been in residence at this joyous season. Lady Gwen proclaimed it a holiday for all belonging to the establishment and mirth and enjoyment became the order of the day. At 2 pm cloths were laid on the tables in the hall and over sixty servants, and in the case of males employed on the estate, their wives, sat down to an excellent dinner. The cloths having been removed, wine and beer arrived *ad libitum* and toasts, sentiments and songs followed in profusion. Some time later the Amlwch Conservative Brass Band marched up to the house and was acknowledged by Sir Arundel and Lady Gwen from the library window. The bandsmen were invited in, and also enjoyed an exceptional dinner. (With the servants having been given a holiday, I wonder who was cooking all these dinners – and washing up?!) The hall having been cleared:

> singing and dancing began in right good earnest and was kept up until about 9 pm when Sir Arundel and Lady

Gwen and their house guests entered and were received with every demonstration of gladness and respect.

They were highly pleased with the way everyone was enjoying themselves and joined in many of the songs and choruses. Some time after 9 pm all 120 guests partook of the feast of the day – the tables actually groaning under the abundance of savoury and delicious dainties placed upon them. Space precluded *The North Wales Chronicle* reporter describing the proceedings which ensued, but he thought it sufficient to comment that they were carried out with great éclat and to the satisfaction of everyone present!

Some days later Amlwch school children were invited to come to see the huge tree, which had been decorated and covered with presents by the domestic staff. Every kindness was shown to the children – they enjoyed themselves beyond measure, and of course each went home clutching a present from the tree.

Just one year later, in **1877** Sir Arundel died.

In **1879** a small vessel was wrecked practically on Lady Gwen's doorstep. She refused to go to bed until she had been assured that the four hands had been rescued, even though this was not until 3 am. She arranged for the sailors to be accommodated in a cottage on her estate for as long as was necessary, and ensured that nutritious meals were delivered to them with clockwork regularity.

The same year Lady Gwen won a prize at Anglesey Agricultural Show with a short horned heifer over two years of age. Interestingly, there was a prize for the servant who had served for the longest consecutive time at a farm, and this went to Ellen Hughes for twenty-eight years at Nantglyn, Amlwch.

In **1880** Lady Gwen donated land for a new school and school house to be built at Pensarn

The Pavilion, Caernarfon

The same year Lord Salisbury (then leader of the Conservative Party, later PM) visited Caernarfonshire for a meeting at The Pavilion, Caernarfon, which Lady Gwen attended. People started queuing at 2.30 knowing that the doors would not open until 4.30 and by 5 pm the hall was full to overflowing. The meeting got off to a rousing start with *Rule Britannia*, followed by Lord Salisbury speaking at length on many topics. Afterwards a procession of 200 people carrying lighted torches proceeded out of the hall behind three brass bands. They passed portraits of Lord Salisbury and Mr. Assheton-Smith – part of a panoramic exhibition in the window of Gwenlyn Evans' Printers. Portraits of other notable locals were visible by lime-light, and the illuminated fountain in Castle Square looked absolutely magnificent. Caernarfon Castle twinkled with fairy lights and 100 rockets were set off. After Lord Salisbury had left with Mr. Assheton-Smith, more fireworks were set off from the castle and new pier, as well as 100 more rockets! There was a massive bonfire on Twthill and numerous businesses and houses were illuminated. Lots more were decked with flags and there was a triumphal arch at the entrance to the town. The following night the Irish Mail train stopped at Menai Bridge to allow Lord Salisbury to board and travel in his private saloon, back to London.

In **1881** there was a Grand Bazaar at Beaumaris Town Hall in aid of the Penmon and Llangoed National School. The room was beautifully decorated with bunting and flags and the individual stalls were also very attractively presented, these included: china – from single pieces to whole dinner services (the latter contributed by Lady Gwen), decorative and useful clothing and furnishings, all manner of flowers and plants, and a bran tub Lucky Dip. A family of sleek, purring kittens curled up in a basket were raffled, as well as a piglet and a small Welsh pony. At the end of the sale, any remaining items were rapidly auctioned off by Mr. Preston of Lleiniog Castle, whose servants had most efficiently served refreshments throughout the two days.

Also this year, Lady Gwen reviewed the rents of her tenants and reduced them by ten percent. She supplied bread for a month for 150 of the poorest labourers and miners, this being in addition to the fifty loaves she already supplied every Saturday to the most deserving local families.

In **1884** Dinorben marble and stone quarries were being opened up and this was warmly welcomed, particularly due to the fact that the closing of the copper mines had led to a lot of unemployment in the Amlwch area. Capt. H. Farnsby-Mills took over the quarries and to demonstrate the quality of the marble, he had a table made – the top of which was inlaid with 400 separate pieces. This then went on display in a shop window in Beaumaris and generated enormous interest. There was a natural harbour close by and a stone pier was being erected to facilitate dispatch by steamer. It was anticipated that 150 quarrymen would be employed initially and that this number would increase significantly over time. Lady Gwen owned the freehold.

In **1885** Lady Gwen was asked to form a ladies' committee to support the work of the Lifeboat Institution, she immediately agreed and started planning for a Lifeboat Saturday.

This was an election year. The results were: R. Davies (Lib) 4,412, and Captain G. Pritchard-Rayner (Con) 3,462. This was a huge disappointment to the Conservatives in Amlwch as they considered that their candidate was very popular and had stood a good chance of winning. They believed he had been defeated by the powerful Methodist congregations in Beaumaris, Llangefni and Holyhead who had equated Mr. Davies with salvation, and Captain Pritchard-Rayner with perdition! A Holyhead newspaper reporter then alleged that Lady Gwen had required her tenants to vote Conservative and that this was why they had done so well in Amlwch – although obviously not so well elsewhere. This was strongly repudiated by Lady Gwen's supporters who made it clear that she had advised her tenants to vote according to their consciences – as indeed she herself would do.

In **1886** Lady Gwen gave a sum of money for the renovation and improvement of the building in which the Primrose League was to meet after its imminent inauguration. She also presented the league with a truly magnificent banner which had its first outing in the opening procession. This turned out to be a great occasion with masses of bunting and many arches and mottoes put up around the town, a particularly pretty one read:

Success to the Primrose League

and was worked in leaves on a white ground by the young

daughter of Mr. Hughes, the Stationmaster. Mr. John Hughes (Frondeg) paid for all the decorations and evening illuminations. The procession was led by the Penrhyn Royal Brass Band, followed by Amlwch school-children, carriages full of gentry including Lady Gwen, and 500 league members wearing their Primrose badges. It paused outside the Conservative Working Men's Club and Mr. John Hughes read the warrant for the formation of the habitation. The assembly was then addressed by Mr. H.C. Raikes MP, Postmaster General, who praised Lady Gwen and Councillor F. Fanning-Evans (Mona Lodge), for all their support of the Conservative cause which had now virtually wiped out the Radicals in Amlwch. It was estimated that 1,800 people joined the march around Amlwch before enjoying a picnic of plum cake and tea provided by the local Conservative Working Men's Club, in a field adjoining the Dinorben Cottage Hospital. After tea, swimming, sports competitions and games were arranged, followed by a band concert; whilst a large contingent of gentry, including Lady Gwen, attended a banquet at the Dinorben Arms

Amlwch Soup Kitchen organisers

The same year the 8th Anglesey Horticultural Show was held, intended to encourage the growing of fruit and vegetables, particularly amongst cottagers.

There was a very severe winter in 1886. Both miners and fishermen were unable to work for weeks on end and they were soon joined by agricultural workers. Coal was distributed, as well as warm clothes and bedding by the Dorcas Society. Members decided that what was needed was a Soup Kitchen, and this was established at the Dinorben Cottage Hospital. A new boiler was bought, and the very best ingredients used to ensure that the soup was nutritious, yet cost only one penny for two pints to the recipients. The Penny Reading Committee provided bread. The popularity of skating was also mentioned with every icy pond and lake crowded!

In **1887** HM Queen Victoria's Golden Jubilee was celebrated in the Amlwch area with a lengthy procession led by the town's Conservative Brass Band, and a street party in Pensarn paid for by Lady Gwen. All were invited – regardless of class, religion or political persuasion. After three cheers for Lady Gwen it was emphasised that she was an unfailing friend to the poor and that no want, distress, or suffering was ever brought to her attention without aid being forth-coming whether in the form of bedding, clothing, food, fuel, or medical help.

Also in 1887 Lady Gwen was a patroness of the first Primrose League Ball to be held in Wales – at the Masonic Hall, Bangor. At 8.30 pm the star over the entrance was illuminated and quite a crowd gathered to watch the arrivals. After the National Anthem, dancing commenced and continued until 4 am accompanied by Mr. Richardson's Band from Liverpool. Supper was provided by Mr. Dudley Dance of the George Hotel.

And Lady Gwen supported two notable efforts to help

the poor – namely the re-opening of a daily Soup Kitchen at Dinorben Cottage Hospital during the winter months; and the intention of Mr. Richard Morgan, The Ragged School's master, to open a weekly Sunday School in a comfortable room in his home. This was for the very poorest children who did not attend a Church Sunday School, and they were to be provided with a hot dinner afterwards. At Christmas they had prime beef and bun-loaf and went home with a bag containing a new testament, an item of warm clothing, a Christmas card, nuts and oranges. Lady Gwen also provided fifty yards each of wincey(ette) and calico for the girls to make into under-garments.

In **1888** Coastguardsman, James Smith, was moved after eight years in Amlwch, to Bangor. This was very much regretted as he was noted not only for his good manners and the preciseness with which he carried out his duties, but also for the fact that he possessed an excellent singing voice and was much in demand for concerts. He was always willing to help with a good song and invariably came off stage a great favourite. Lady Gwen gave him a substantial leaving gift in gratitude for his services – guarding the coast and vocal!

The same year interested parties were invited by Mr. T. Fanning-Evans, the lessee, to see the work being carried out at Mona and Parys Mountain Copper Mines. The visit was followed by a meal at which toasts were proposed in their absence to the lessors, Lady Gwen and the 4th Marquess of Anglesey. Mr. Fanning-Evans had been Her Majesty's first Inspector of Metalliferous Mines in Wales before coming to Amlwch, and he believed that Mona and Parys Mountain were ahead of nearly every other mine in Britain with regard to management and production. Mr. Fanning-Evans commented on the good business relationship he enjoyed with the lessors, and assured everyone of his intention to continue to protect and improve the lives of the miners.

Also in 1888, as a result of the village having undergone a complete change of political allegiance, a Conservative Working Men's Club was formed in Pensarn. Lady Gwen had given the premises in which the club met, free of rent and other expenses, and allowed the venue to be altered to suit the needs of the club. She also contributed generously to club funds, provided a bagatelle board and books, funds for the purchase of instruments for a proposed Brass Band and continued to take a lively interest in its activities. The Band was soon formed, and later in the year members were entertained to a splendid banquet at Mona Lodge by Mr. and Mrs. Fanning-Evans. After the meal and toasts, loyal and patriotic songs were sung. It was noted that scurrilous information concerning the club published in a Welsh half-penny paper (read by Liberal supporters), far from having the desired effect, had only succeeded in attracting new members to the Conservatives!

That summer Lady Gwen attended a garden party at Penrhyn Castle, with catering by Bollands of Chester.

Still in 1888, Lady Gwen reduced rents by fifteen percent in recognition of the depression in agriculture and trade, and paid off the outstanding debt on the Ragged School.

And finally that year the Menai Habitation of the Primrose League held a brilliant Ball for 180 guests at the George Hotel, Bangor Ferry. Due to the huge success of the previous year's ball they had to move to a more spacious venue, where there was a splendid ballroom and a suite of rooms for the use of guests. This event was supported by Lady Gwen. The hotel's grand piano was moved onto the stage and music was supplied by Mr. Richardson's Band. The decorations were spectacular – the entrance and arches were draped with red velvet and festooned with Primroses, and corridors were lined with Palms and exotic plants twinkling with fairy lights. In fact fairy lights and Chinese lanterns were everywhere, and coloured lamps nestled amongst the evergreens on mantelpieces and surrounding the massive pier glasses (mirrors). In the ballroom the walls were draped with flags, banners and garlands of Holly; bannerettes were suspended from the ceiling, there was red, white and blue bunting, and the beautiful Mostyn banner of blue velvet hand-painted with Primroses had pride of place. Catering was by Mr. Dudley Dance who owned the hotel, the theme was recherché fruits of the season and even the menu cards were decorated with Primroses. Dancing started a little after 9 pm and continued until 5 am but in the spacious conservatory there were lots of comfortable sofas where guests could rest.

In **1892** Lady Gwen gave sheets, blankets and quilts for the beds provided for ship-wrecked or destitute sailors at the Sailor's Rest, Amlwch Ragged School.

The same year Lady Gwen and other landowners unsuccessfully tried to restrict the use of the foreshore at Cemlyn Bay. As a result there was a celebratory demonstration to thank Mr. Owen Williams, the nominal defendant, and Messrs. Owen and Griffith, Bangor, the solicitors who had acted for him in the legal proceedings.

Also in 1892 Lady Gwen supported a concert in Amlwch Assembly Rooms in aid of the Temperance Movement. Amlwch held its own Musical Eisteddfod and an Art, Industrial and Loan Exhibition of which Lady Gwen was a patron. There were 360 entries for the competition held in the Board Schoolrooms. Classes included brass repousse (chased) work, iron-work, wood-carving, farm and garden produce, cooking, plain and fancy needlework, drawing and painting etc. Well over 700 items were loaned for the exhibition, including a carved chair which dated from 1292 and was reputed to have belonged to Prince Llewelyn. The rooms had been beautifully decorated with banners, the most appropriate motto being:

Whatsoever things are pure, whatsoever things are lovely – think on these things.

In **1893** the tenants of the Llys Dulas estate and other well-wishers contributed 50 guineas to buy a carriage clock for Miss Gwen Mary Neave on her 21st birthday. This was purchased from Mr. Daniel Jones, Watchmaker, of Amlwch. The town had been extensively decorated with banners, bunting and flags. The Misses Williams' London House was noted as being particularly pretty with no time, trouble, or expense spared and the motto:

Long life to Miss Neave

worked in flowers and leaves. The Chinese Lanterns and Venetian Lights in the evening brought hundreds of spectators into the town. There were fireworks in Dinorben Square and bonfires blazed on surrounding hills. Lady Gwen sent 170 lbs. of tea to be distributed amongst the poor women in Amlwch. Mr. Lewis Hughes wrote some verses to commemorate the occasion, ending with:

Though fires that crown each joyous hill
This night, but burn to smoulder,
Affection will keep burning still
And never will grow colder.

Also in 1893 on the occasion of a Royal Visit by HRH Prince Edward (later Edward VII) and HRH Princess Alexandra, Prince and Princess of Wales, a tea party was given for children attending the Ragged School and sixty other poor children from Amlwch. Each child received an item of clothing from Lady Gwen. This year she also provided complete bales of calico and melton (a woollen cloth with a felt-like appearance), for the girls in the sewing class to make up into garments.

In **1894**, the second of the twice yearly collections of rents from the Llys Dulas estate took place as usual at the Dinorben Arms, but supervised for the first time in the absence of Lady Gwen, by her sons Thomas and Arundel. The tradition of a splendid dinner being provided at the hotel for the tenants was honoured, and the farmers spent a most pleasant evening with the two young gentlemen.

The same year Lady Gwen invited all the members of the Amlwch Habitation of the Primrose League to a Fête at Llys Dulas. Despite drenching rain, 400-500 people arrived – Liberals as well as Conservatives were welcomed by Lady Gwen, and entertained in the beautifully decorated Great Hall by music performed on the harp, pianoforte and violin. Mr. John Hughes then spoke about the Primrose League. At 3 pm the first hundred were served tea in the dining hall – with a spread of every imaginable delicacy, and this was replenished for each subsequent sitting.

The fête stalls were highly decorated and had all manner of beautiful things for sale, many of which had been donated by Lady Gwen. It was considered that the huge success was due in no small measure to Lady Gwen's presence throughout the whole three days – helping out wherever needed and chatting happily to everyone, as well as discreetly providing items of clothing for those in need. By the close on Saturday it was sold out! It was well over twenty years since a fête had been held in Amlwch, and that was in 1867 for the restoration of St. Eleth's Church. In the evening balloons were sent up followed by fireworks, thus rounding off three most enjoyable days.

Also in 1894 Lady Gwen became a patron of Lady Augusta Mostyn's Gwynedd Ladies' Art Society which met at the Round Room (Conway Cockpit), until the opening of the Mostyn Gallery, Llandudno, specifically to allow ladies to exhibit their art.

In **1895** Sir Thomas Neave reached his twenty-first birthday and there were great celebrations in Amlwch, the streets being thronged with people. A presentation committee took numerous and costly gifts up to Llys Dulas and were invited to lunch. After lunch, Sir Thomas and Lady Gwen proceeded by carriage into town following the Amlwch Conservative Brass Band. Sir Thomas' brother and sister followed in a second carriage. An illuminated address was presented to Sir Thomas, after which there was a bicycle race and sports. In the evening there were fireworks and mention was particularly made of how beautiful London House looked – lit outside with a myriad of lamps; and the fact that the Golden Goat Hotel had two live goats on a section of the roof.

The same year Lady Gwen's annual gift of a Christmas Tree for Amlwch Ragged School reached the ceiling and was laden with all kinds of fancy and useful articles. These were distributed by Lady Gwen, assisted by other local ladies.

In **1896** an Exhibition of Wood Carving produced at Mr. Henley's classes, was held in Amlwch Literary and Scientific Hall, and opened by Lady Gwen. With her encouragement this led to the formation of the Anglesey Industries Association – to encourage the revival of old industries (also supported by Col. Cotton). There were seventeen women exhibitors and only two men. The carving on four large screen panels by Miss Mitchell was exceptionally fine

The same year there was a Lifeboat Demonstration in Amlwch which attracted hundreds of visitors. The thirteen crewmen were very smartly dressed in their red caps, blue tunics and cork jackets. Their boat was drawn by seventeen fine heavy horses, their manes and tails trimmed for the occasion. The procession was led by a brass band. They paused in Dinorben Square, and amongst much cheering, Mr. John Hughes made an appeal for the Lifeboat Institution. Lady Gwen, as local president, was present and took a great interest in the proceedings.

At 3 pm on a perfect June day in **1897** 200 children from Pensarn Board School, each wearing a Queen Victoria's Diamond Jubilee Medal donated by Lady Gwen, and some waving flags, marched up the lawn to Llys Dulas, preceded by Cemaes Volunteer Band. Awaiting them, under the trees, were long tables laden with all manner of edibles and urns of tea. Grace having been sung, the children set to in earnest and soon there was not a morsel left. It was then the turn of the band to take tea, and finally Lady Gwen, her daughter and helpers. Sports followed – the prizes donated and presented by Lady Gwen. Then a multitude of pretty balloons floated up into the air, their progress watched with delight by children and adult helpers alike. Before they left, Lady Gwen presented each child with a Jubilee Mug with dual portraits of Her Majesty in 1837 and 1897, and a bag containing a bun, an orange and some nuts. The National Anthem was played and three hearty cheers given for Her Majesty, then three for Lady Gwen and Miss Neave and finally three for their helpers. In the evening there was a firework display.

In **1899** Lady Gwen took an interest in a coal field which was being developed at Malltreath Marsh.

The same year Amlwch's Chrysanthemum Society held a show of flowers and birds at the Victoria Drill Hall in Caernarfon. Lady Gwen won first prizes in the Chrysanthemums and Tomatoes Classes.

Also in 1899 Lady Gwen attended a meeting called by Lord and Lady Penrhyn at Penrhyn Castle concerning the Society for the Protection of Waifs and Strays (also supported by Mrs. and Miss Clegg) and what could be done to help them.

In **1900** Lady Gwen sent a letter of apology for being unable to attend a meeting regarding Anglesey Industries. The ladies present were shown examples of linseys (fabrics woven with a linen warp and woollen weft), and silk and woollen materials woven in Anglesey's pandys (mills), of which by that time there were eight. The ladies also saw vegetable dyes used to colour the fabrics. And it was decided to hold their first exhibition, including children's work, at New Hall, Menai Bridge. Donations of goods and money for prizes were to be sought.

At Christmas the children at the Ragged School had their annual treat. This year it took the form of sixty handsome books being presented as prizes, followed by a good hot dinner of roast beef, rabbit pie, plum pudding, cakes and tea. Before they left there were three cheers for the Princess of Wales who had supplied a hamper of rabbits for the occasion, three for the Neave family who had supplied everything else, and three more for Lieutenant Arundel Neave, Lady Gwen's younger son, who was en route from India to South Africa with the 16th Lancers.

In **1902** Amlwch was gaily decorated for the return from the Boer War of Lieut. Arundel Neave. His train was met at the station by a welcoming party and they proceeded, led by Llangefni Brass Band, to the Dinorben Arms for lunch. By the early afternoon a huge crowd of tenants and well-wishers had assembled around the stage which had been erected outside the hotel, to watch the presentation of a sword of honour and illuminated address to Lieutenant Neave. The sword had a mother-of-pearl handle, a finely chased gold guard, was richly decorated with gold and silver and inscribed:

> To: Lieutenant Arundel Neave from his friends and well wishers.

After the presentation, 1,000 school children were treated to tea at the Assembly Rooms and in the evening the crowds returned to watch a firework display set off beside the Coastguard Station.

In **1902** Amlwch's own Horticultural Society held its first show at the Board School, Lady Gwen being the patron. There were over 300 exhibits. Lady Gwen's gardener won sixteen first prizes!

In **1903** Amlwch held its second Annual Flower, Fruit and Vegetable Show at the National School, under the patronage of Lady Gwen. There were about 400 entries for five classes: professional gardeners, amateur gardeners, farmers and cottagers, miscellaneous, and cottagers living within three miles of Amlwch. The first prize of the Toogood Challenge Shield (presented by Toogood's Seeds of Southampton) was won by Lady Gwen's gardener.

In **1904** Miss Neave, daughter of Lady Gwen was the Lady Patroness of the Anglesey Hunt, Major H. Hughes (almost certainly her uncle or cousin) of Kinmel Park being the Comptroller.

Ball Suppers were still held at the Williams-Bulkeley Arms Hotel and the Balls at Beaumaris Town Hall but the supper menus had become even more extensive.

Music was by the Blue Hungarian Band, there were three supper dances, barn dances, gallops, several sets of The Lancers, polkas and waltzes.

The same year Lady Gwen attended Royal Welsh Yacht Club Ball at the Royal Sportsman's Hotel, Caernarfon attended by 450 guests. The ballroom was decorated with flags arranged to form well known nautical signals running from floor to ceiling, evergreens, garlands of flowers and Palms. The women's dresses were exquisitely colourful, contrasting with the dark dinner suits of the men. Music by Mr. Clayton's band from Liverpool included a gallop – John Peel, leading up to supper which was served at midnight. The supper room ceiling was decorated with green, pink, red and yellow streamers and electric light, and bunting and flowers garlanded the walls. A presentation of a silver salver was made to Mr. Charles Jones in appreciation of his thirty-three years as secretary. Mr. Jones commented that the years he had spent with the club were the happiest of his life

Menu:
Dressed Lobster with salad   Mayonnaissie of Salmon,
Pressed Beef   Boar's Head   York Hams   Ox Tongues
Boned, Truffled Turkeys
Galantine of Chickens in Aspic   Galantine of Veal
Roast Beef   Roast Chickens   Chicken a la Bechamel,
Petits Bouches   Veal and Ham Pies
Benedictine and Bohemian Creams
Danzig, Mosaic and Wine Jellies,
Eclaires du Chocolat   French Pastries   Ices   Log Cakes
Madelines
Russian Imperial Cake

Catering was by Mr. and Mrs. Crispin and 150 people were seated at each of three sittings. Dancing resumed after supper and continued for several hours, and finally ... soups were offered on leaving the Ball.

In **1905** Lady Gwen was involved in a dispute about a right of way which crossed in front of Llys Dulas, leading to the headland and shore. It was decided that she had unlawfully obstructed the path.

Like Lady Hughes-Hunter, Lady Gwen was concerned about coastal erosion and in **1907** she applied to the Board of Trade to issue an order banning the carting away of sand, shingle and seaweed from the beach at Porth Eilian. She had testimony from lighthouse keepers that the road leading to Point Lynas Lighthouse was seriously imperiled and the beach had sunk six feet in eleven years. Lady Gwen contended that valuable agricultural and building land was being washed away, and the loss of sand was making the beach less attractive to visitors.

In **1914** Lady Gwen appealed for Christmas gifts for the soldiers guarding the Menai Bridge under the direction of her son, Major Sir Thomas Neave, saying that she would personally receive and acknowledge gifts. The Bishop of Bangor and Mrs. Williams sent tables and benches, and 100 cups, saucers, plates, and sets of cutlery for the rest room. (Other gifts are detailed in Lady Hughes-Hunter's entry).

In **1915** Lady Gwen opposed an order for the compulsory leasing of 150 acres of her farmland for allotments but was defeated.

The same year Lady Gwen's second son, Major Arundel, died as a result of injuries sustained at the Battle of Ypres. The news of his death cast a deep gloom over Amlwch as he was very well known and a great favourite. A Memorial Service was held at Llanwenllwyfo Church. He was buried in Ypres Town Cemetery.

Also in 1915 Sir Thomas and Lady Gwen ensured that the wounded soldiers at Bodlondeb Military Hospital had as happy a Christmas as possible.

In **1916** Lady Gwen died. Her funeral was held at her home, Llys Dulas. Despite very stormy weather it was attended by all classes of the community, which testified to the high esteem and deep affection in which Lady Gwen was held. She was buried in Llanwenllwyfo Churchyard. In her will she bequeathed £200 to each of her two maids and £500 to her butler, also £60 to her cook and one year's wages to each servant who had been in her employment for at least two years.

Lady Dorina Lockhart NEAVE (nèe **Clifton**) was born in 1880, the daughter of Sir George Herbert and Pamela. She married Sir Thomas Lewis Hughes Neave, 5th Baronet, and they had two sons and two daughters.

In **1909** on the occasion of her marriage, Lady Dorina was presented at Court at Buckingham Palace. She wore a gown of ivory duchesse satin with a corsage of old Brussels lace, the skirt was slashed to reveal a cascade of the same lace. A matching satin train edged with lace was attached to the shoulders and her ornaments were diamonds.

In **1916** Lady Dorina set up a fund to pay for postage for parcels to be sent to Anglesey soldiers serving in Turkey, as many families simply could not afford the cost of stamps.

Turkey was close to Lady Dorina's heart. Her maternal grand-father, Henry Cumberbatch, was a diplomat who had served in Turkey for many years. Dorina was brought up there and wrote extensively about the country, most notably three books entitled: *Remembering Kut, Twenty-six years on the Bosphorus and The Romance of the Bosphorus.*

In **1918** there was a great deal of concern when Sir Thomas proposed increasing rents. The tenants stressed to their Anglesey Farmer's Union that they had always enjoyed good relations with the estate, but they did not think this was an opportune time for the landowner to be considering increasing their rents, and in turn their union put this to Sir Thomas. The outcome was not recorded.

The same year Amlwch Mother's Union was formed with Lady Dorina as president.

She had not been at all impressed when she arrived in England, the buildings, parks, horse-buses:

like advertising carts belonging to a circus,

hunting, village sports, and even the Alhambra Music Hall were all well below her expectations! But she did grow to love Dagnam Park, her husband's family seat in Essex and was inconsolable when, after WW2, the Labour Government slapped a compulsory purchase order on it and re-developed the site for housing. Lady Dorina died in 1955 and was buried in the cemetery attached to St. Thomas's Church, Noak Hill, London.

Pilgrimage for Peace

In 1926, under the auspices of the North Wales Women's Peace Council (NWWPC), and inspired by the 1913 Suffragist's *Votes for Women* Pilgrimage, it was decided to organise a Peace Pilgrimage to promote conciliation and arbitration in place of war:

Law not War

was its slogan.

So many women had lost fathers, brothers, husbands and fiancés in WW1 or seen them return with terrible physical and mental scars that understandably, they were terrified of there being another war, and intended to do everything in their power to prevent it happening. The main protagonists in North Wales were Mrs. Silyn Roberts MA from Blaenau Ffestiniog and Mrs. Gwladys Thoday BA. from Llanfairfechan, joint secretaries of the NWWPC and Mrs. Charlotte Price White from Bangor its chairman.

On 27 May the North Wales Pilgrimage began at **Pen-y-groes** near Caernarfon. Processions from: Morfa Bychan, Nefin, Pwllheli, Criccieth, Bettws Garmon, Rhostryfan, Rhosgadfan, Waenfawr, Llanellhaiarn, Llanllechid, Carmel, Nantle and Llanlyfni joined the Pen-y-Groes procession; resulting in 2,000 women striding through this small market town with their blue peace banners and flags held aloft. No wonder it made such an impact!

From Pen-y-groes they made their way to **Groeslon**, then on to **Caernarfon** where Llanberis, Ebenezer, Pentir and Douglas Hill joined; then on to **Port Dinorwig** to meet up with Tal-y-sarn, Bontnewydd, Bala Deulyn, Llithfaen and Clynog.

Capel Curig, Ogwen Valley, Tregarth, Bethesda, Penrhos Garnedd, Llandegai, Benllech and Porthaethwy joined at **Bangor**. The next places on the route were **Llanfairfechan** where Aber joined, then **Penmaenmawr** and **Conwy** where the numbers were swelled by contingents from Penmachno, Dolwyddelan, Betws-y-coed, Trefriw, Llanrwst, Llanbedrycennin, Tal-y-bont, Ro-wen, Gyffin, Llandudno and Llandudno Junction.

From there they made their way to **Mochdre**, **Colwyn Bay** where Penrhos (College) joined, and on to **Rhyl**, **Prestatyn**, **Holywell**, **Llangollen** and **Chester**.

It was reported that everywhere, they were welcomed with interest and enthusiasm – unlike the NUWSS pilgrims who encountered some frightening hostility. They were frequently asked to speak about the purpose of the Pilgrimage – even in tiny villages. Wherever they stopped, the peace resolution was read, hymns were sung in Welsh and English and prayers for peace offered. The resolution was as follows:

> We, members and supporters of the Peace Maker's Pilgrimage, believing that law should take the place of war in the settlement of international disputes, urge His Majesty's Government to agree to submit all disputes to conciliation or arbitration, and, by taking the lead in the proposed Disarmament Conference of the League of Nations Union, show that Great Britain does not intend to appeal to force.

The names of every town, village and organisation which supported the resolution were inscribed on flags (**including Caernarfonshire Council of WI's**).

At Bangor the speakers were: The Bishop of Bangor, Rev. George Maitland Davies (ex-MP for the University of Wales), Mr. Cynan Albert Evans Jones – *Cynan the Bard*, Mr. Elias Henry Jones (League of Nations Union), the local Rabbi and Mrs. Charlotte Price White. The women placed wreaths of Laurel and Daffodils (the League of Nations flower) tied with blue ribbon (the colour of peace and of the Pilgrimage), at the North Wales Heroes Memorial and the town's War Memorial.

On 28 May they started to make their way along the coast. It must have brought back so many memories for Mrs. Price White – who had walked all the way from Bangor to London on the NUWSS Pilgrimage thirteen years earlier. At Penmaenmawr Mrs. Owen Owen of Tan-y-foel (and Owen-Owen's Department Store, Liverpool) entertained the pilgrims to lunch. At Conwy the number of pilgrims reached its maximum when the sixty women who had travelled from Bangor were joined by eleven other contingents. The Llandudno group had been organised by Mrs. Humphrey Evans BA (League of Nations Union). Between forty and fifty women met at the Town Hall waving blue pennons and flying their flag, and were conveyed by charabanc via Mostyn Street and Conway Road to Conway. The reporter at this meeting portrayed it as:

> Surely the most picturesque on the route: it was an inspiring sight to see the procession winding its way along the battlements, and when the banners and flags were laid down, the women forming themselves into orderly rows around and before the platform which had been set up in the old banqueting hall.

The North Wales Peace Pilgrimage at Conway

The Mayor, Mr. Harker, gave a civic welcome and Mrs. Price White read the resolution for conciliation and arbitration – which was carried unanimously. The assembled crowd was then addressed in Welsh, in a most stirring manner, by Mrs. Lloyd Jones of Criccieth. She had been the organiser of the *Memorial to America* signed by 390,296 women in Wales in 1923-24, urging their American sisters to persuade the US Senate to become a full member of the League of Nations Union, to safeguard peace for future generations.

Rev. George Maitland Davies and Mr. E.H. Jones spoke again and finally *Cynan* drew a vivid picture of the ruins of Conway Castle and all that they stood for – armed power having failed the world and the need for another way to be found. He quoted the Welsh saying that the sword was only to be honoured when it was lying idle and tarnished. The speech was all the more moving knowing that *Cynan* had served with the military in WW1. Many photographs were taken and twice the procession was filmed. Tea was provided in Conway.

At this point, all but six of the Caernarfonshire women left for home, but the Llandudno contingent and those who had come to Conwy from the surrounding villages continued to Colwyn Bay and met up with their group. A huge crowd gathered for a meeting on the beach. The reporter commented that it made him realise what a great concept the Pilgrimage was, how – just as in the case of the NUWSS Pilgrimage, it arrested the attention of people who could not have been reached in any other way.

On 29 May another Colwyn Bay meeting was addressed by Miss Cecile Matheson (Board of Arbitration), Mrs. Lloyd Jones, and local women: Mrs. Gwladys Thoday, Mrs. Silyn Roberts and Mrs. Charlotte Price White; as were those at Rhyl, Prestatyn and Holywell.

On 30 May alas, the pilgrims got lost beyond Prestatyn and were delayed for an hour before arriving at Holywell, but were still greeted by patient crowds and held a most successful meeting.

Late that afternoon one car left for Llangollen, the

The North Wales Peace Pilgrimage at Rhyl

occupants intending to support a meeting there that evening.

On 31 May nine Welsh pilgrims, under the North Wales banner, met up with the Birkenhead and Wirral, and Chester contingents to walk to Chester Town Hall Square. This gathering was addressed by Councillor Phyllis Brown and Miss Matheson, the three North Wales women, and finally by Mrs. Paget, wife of the Bishop of Chester. Councillor Brown said that most people present would have vivid memories of the Great War, but those who did not actually take part in it would do well to do what she had been doing – read books written by men who had taken part. One such man had written:

> It is time the nations found some more reasonable way of settling their disputes than by sending a population as large as London into an area as large as Wales to spend several years attempting to destroy each other by mechanical means.

Many men who fought did so, she continued, because they hoped it would be a war to end war, but there was not yet the feeling of peace and security in Europe, which they were all hoping for.

Mrs. Gwladys Thoday spoke about the wonderful enthusiasm the Pilgrimage had aroused throughout North Wales and added:

> It is clear to me that if we do not end war, war will end us.

She then asked every woman present to take on the responsibility of working for peace.

Mrs. Graham spoke on behalf of the Wirral contingent, and said she believed that at the next election, the only question which should be asked of candidates would be:

Are you in favour of peace?

She continued that nothing else mattered anyway, if they were going to be blown to smithereens in a few years. It was not sufficient to pass a resolution for peace – they must work for it with might and main. She thought apathy had contributed largely to WW1. They must teach their children from their earliest infancy to oppose war, and eliminate everything which encouraged a military state of mind – such as toy soldiers. Mrs. Graham closed by saying that it was eight years since the end of WW1. The people of Britain had been very patient but they were losing patience. Seventeen countries had already signed the Arbitration Clause but Britain had not. It was lagging behind – not leading, and that was a shameful thing for an Empire of such might and such power. She re-iterated that if they wanted peace they must work for it. If they did not work for peace they would get war, and it would be their apathy which would be responsible.

Mrs. Burden from Moreton said she had taken part in the 1913 Pilgrimage and here she was again. She appealed particularly to the mothers of Chester, to support the cause of Peace.

Miss Matheson then referred at length to arbitration methods used to address industrial issues and made a plea for the same processes to be applied to international affairs.

The closing speech was by Mrs. Paget, who explained that she was a Justice of the Peace and was bound so far as she could, to keep the King's peace and to keep it justly. But she was a Christian, bound to keep the peace for a far higher King, a more universal King, a King who was Lord and God of all the nations on earth; and saw everyone as equal. She concluded that she spoke too as the mother of a son who had lost his life fighting for his country, and because she wished to carry on his work – honestly done, in a peaceful spirit, to its ultimate conclusion of World Peace. Mrs. Paget then moved a resolution for peace, which was carried unanimously by the vast crowd.

Afterwards they walked the short distance to the War Memorial on Cathedral Green, where Samuel James Paget's name was recorded, Mrs. Paget laid a laurel wreath on behalf of the pilgrims and they sang the hymn: *Oh God our help in ages past ...*

At this distance, we can only imagine Mrs. Paget's feelings, and doubtless the feelings of many others present who had lost loved ones in WW1, when they reached the verse:

> Time like an ever rolling stream
> Bears all its sons away,
> They fly forgotten, as a dream
> Dies at the opening day.

I am sure she, and they, never forgot.

The Pilgrimage was designed in relays – each group eventually handing over to the next contingent waiting to take the message forward.

Some of the banners were particularly memorable:
One in stark black and white depicting a woman gazing at the crosses in a war cemetery;
A chubby little boy playing Soldiers with the words: *The Unknown Warrior,*
A futuristic depiction of aeroplanes raining destruction on homes and civilians, and
perhaps most shockingly, a mother holding a baby with the words *Cannon Fodder.*

At one village, pilgrims were handed a bunch of cottage garden flowers with the message:

May your peace efforts succeed.

A wounded soldier commented that it was too late for him, but he still wished them well.

And when two footsore pilgrims boarded a London bus for the last stage of their journey, the conductor refused to take their fare – saying he would pay it for them.

On 19 June an estimated 100,000 women in four processions from The Embankment, Kensington, Maida

A leader of a section of the Peace Pilgrimage in London

Vale, and Bloomsbury converged on Hyde Park. The sun shone and the leafy green of early summer emphasised the sea of blue streaming into the park. Each procession was headed by a woman on horseback, wearing a black and silver three-cornered cockade hat and a long blue mantle on which a silver dove of peace had been hand-painted. One of these four women was Sybil Thorndike (not yet a Dame) leading the Welsh and Cornish pilgrims. Every pilgrim wore a blue arm-band decorated with a white dove and individual group leaders wore blue smocks over their dresses with a dove and the word *Pax* embroidered in silver.

The women from the Guildhouses in Eccleston Square wore their blue cassocks with white ruffled collars. The League of Nations Union carried their multi-coloured national banners, and members of the League of the Church Militant were dressed entirely in the other peace colour – orange, and followed an ecclesiastical cross.

Some women still favoured the Suffragette's **g**reen, **w**hite and **v**iolet (symbolising *give women the vote*, and bearing in mind that women under thirty still were not enfranchised). Graduates in their black gowns with purple and scarlet lined hoods drove in a carriage alongside four miner's wives who had walked all the way from Barnsley. And one woman had walked the whole 500 miles from Aberdeen. At this point the reporter went off at somewhat of a tangent saying that:

> Never has modern London seen such a congregation of women wearing flat-heeled shoes: country walking shoes, Oxford brogues, pumps, rubber shoes for runners, sandals, slippers and tennis shoes – but never a French heel!

One banner carried a name in reverse – as if in disgrace, and that was the name of a beautiful village in Kent,

Lamberhurst, the only place in the whole of England, Scotland and Wales where the resolution for peace had been defeated. Miss Cecilia Preston, who carried the banner commented:

> I don't mind how much its name is broadcast throughout the land. The village had been previously canvassed by well-to-do people who induced the villagers to support them. Even if an archangel had gone to them in the cause of peace, I do not believe that it would have made any difference.

A student from Spurgeon's Theological College joined the procession beating a drum, and explained that he was beating it for peace – not war. And it was noted that the Welsh women sang beautifully as they walked.

There were twenty-eight North Wales women at Hyde Park including Mrs. James Marks and Mrs. T.O. Pierce from Llandudno, Mrs. Silyn Roberts and Mrs. Thoday. Before this final procession, eighty-five resolutions from sixty different towns and villages in North Wales supporting the pilgrims – and peace, had been received. The names of the sixty locations were included on banners proudly carried by those twenty-eight women. Mrs. Thoday was interviewed and remarked that they had been preaching to the converted at indoor meetings, but to the unconverted out of doors – and they had made many converts.

There were twenty-two platforms and some very high-profile speakers, including: Mrs. Elsie Cadbury, Dame Millicent Fawcett, Miss Eleanor Rathbone, Mrs. Margaret Wintringham MP (WI member), Mrs. Silyn Roberts (who spoke in Welsh) and Mrs. Gwladys Thoday.

Lord Parmoor, a lawyer and politician, was the main speaker and said that the movement in favour of arbitration had ebbed since its high watermark in Geneva in 1924, when fifty countries had accepted the protocol. He felt that Britain was not now so far removed from the terrible prospect of another war. There was not the slightest chance of real advance towards disarmament unless Britain took the lead. If the Pilgrimage succeeded in turning the tide and obtaining conciliation or arbitration as a first resort, it would have done a great work.

After the resolution had been proclaimed for the final time, the Pilgrimage closed with a Pageant of children, actors and dancers directed by Mr. Robert Atkins and Miss Alys Buckton who, as the Figure of Peace bearing an olive branch, appeared on a raised dais and received gifts from her children; whilst the World, the Flesh, and the Devil linked together by silken chains stood marvelling at this strange being which had come amongst them. Then came the throwing off by the World of the fetters which had bound it to the Flesh and the Devil, and the presentation by King Arthur of his sword – and the laying upon it an olive branch by Peace. They were joined by the Nine Virtues, Arthurian

Peace Pageant, Hyde Park

Knights, Maids of the Holy Grail and representations of peacemakers from Pythagoras to Livingstone. The spectacle concluded with an utterance by the voice of Pilgrimage:

> Through cities, through villages, through country lanes we pass, bringing thoughts of men. We have nursed the lonely flame on many a hearth. We have kindled forgotten love 'mid smouldering embers of revolt. God's dream for his world, hidden from the beginning, is nearer for this day's deed.

Meetings had been graced by clergy of every denomination, councillors and mayors, politicians of every party, and ordinary men and women – rich and poor alike. The North Wales women looked back on the Pilgrimage with the utmost satisfaction and were full of gratitude for the hospitality and support they had received.

Afterwards the NWWPC continued to campaign for peace. Mrs. Silyn Roberts and Mrs. Gwladys Thoday remained as its Welsh and English speaking secretaries respectively. In 1928 it became affiliated to the Women's International League for Peace and Freedom (WILPF). The same year Frank Kellogg, Secretary of State for the USA asked the governments of France, Germany, Great Britain, Italy, Japan and the USA to renounce war. The NWWPC raised massive support for the Kellogg Pact through meetings held throughout Wales. Miss Balch from Massachusetts spoke at Bangor and Wrexham and women travelled miles to hear her, many being accommodated overnight by local Peace Council members. The NWWPC managed to get 174 resolutions passed urging the government to support the pact, as well as collecting hundreds of thousands of signatures in support. At the 1929 Election, the first at which women under thirty were allowed to vote, members supported candidates who were in favour of disarmament. Women's votes outnumbered men's by over one million. The Kellogg Pact was eventually signed by sixty-four countries.

In 1930 Mrs. Thoday joined a deputation from the Women's Peace Crusade attending the London Naval Conference. They met with Prime Minister, Ramsay MacDonald, and delegates from Australia, Japan, New Zealand and the USA, urging them to honour the Kellogg Pact and reduce naval armaments worldwide. Only two women were actually allowed to speak but one, Mrs. Margery Corbett-Ashby, President of the British Commonwealth League, made special mention of the women of North Wales, their amazing campaign and the resolutions presented that day on their behalf by Mrs. Thoday. It was agreed that ship-building should be restricted until 1936 and that the size of aircraft-carriers and submarines should be limited, but WILPF did not consider that this went nearly far enough:

War is renounced, let us renounce armaments.

By this time the NWWPC was active in all six counties in North Wales, and members of the North Wales branch of WILPF met at various locations on Anglesey, and regularly at Menai Bridge, Bangor, Blaenau Ffestiniog, Colwyn Bay, Deganwy, Llandudno Junction, Llanfairfechan, Penmaen-mawr, Rhyl and Wrexham.

Throughout 1931 the NWWPC directed their efforts towards getting every adult resident in Wales to sign a Disarmament Declaration, which was to be presented to the Geneva Disarmament Conference the following year. Their success can be measured by the fact that they obtained 122,198 signatures: representing one fifth of the population of North Wales. (The 32,394 signatures appended in Caernarfonshire represented a quarter of the population of that county).

In 1932 Mrs. Thoday attended the WILPF Conference at Grenoble and reported on Britain's work towards disarmament. On her return, she spoke in Bangor on: *World Disarmament or World Disaster* and stated that British support for disarmament was increasing. Only the previous week, **10,000 delegates at the WI AGM** in London had passed a resolution in support. Mrs. Thoday ended by expressing WILPF's concern that armaments were being produced by private companies (previously they had been manufactured only at the behest of governments) and huge profits were being made. WILPF had demanded that:

> All private profits from manufactured armaments should cease.

The same year, 1932, Mrs. Price White died and Mrs. Emrys Evans, wife of the Principal of UCNW became NWWPC chairman.

Due to the depression, the NWPCC found it difficult to raise funds during 1933, but in 1934 managed to organise meetings about the traffic in arms, and collected signatures for the League of Nations Union's initiative of a Peace Ballot. Mrs. Thoday attended eight meetings of the WILPF Executive in London. During this year she resigned from the Welsh National Council of the League of Nations Union, but continued to support its local work. In 1936 there were thirty-two peace meetings in North Wales; and in 1937 thirty-eight meetings, a Peace Exhibition in a shop in Menai Bridge and numerous study and discussion circles were held. WILPF also launched the *People's Mandate* international campaign – which was well supported across

North Wales, demanding that governments address the impending crisis in Europe. The same year Mrs. Thoday helped Bangor students to organise a meeting to discuss the situation in Spain, and personally arranged for Senora Camps to attend. The Free Church Council, Communists and Labour were represented but afterwards both Mrs. Thoday and Senora Camps were of the opinion that the meeting had been:

   too red.

Mrs. Thoday was a Liberal as were the majority of NWWPC members, but the organisation was careful to keep its policies broad enough to accommodate Labour supporters as well.

   With the rise of facism in the 1930's the Peace Movement was forced to confront the differences between pacifists and those who believed force to be necessary under certain circumstances. WILPF supported universal disarmament, as did the NWWPC; but the League of Nations Union was in favour of a permanent international armed force and subsequent re-armament.

   With the declaration of war in 1939 the NWWPC's Annual Report posed the question:

   What can the NWWPC and WILPF do in these difficult times? What do we stand for? The official view, confirmed by the majority of us, is that at this moment we believe war in the defence of freedom to be a lesser evil than surrendering the whole of Europe, and especially its youth, to slavery to Nazi principles. We realise that there is another point of view – that taken by honest conscientious objectors and maintained by a strong minority of WILPF – that nothing from without a man can injure him so much as giving up his inward conviction that war is wrong ...

What then can we do? A great deal ... we can work with all our might against the bitterness that will get stronger and stronger as the war goes on; defend the position of the honest conscientious objector, and strive against the anti-German feelings that include all Germans: innocent and guilty, Nazi and refugee, in one blind condemnation.

In 1939 NWWPC branch reports were received from Bangor, Colwyn Bay and Llanrwst. Bangor commented that they had not thought it wise to attempt to hold many meetings that year, but there had been one very successful meeting when the UCNW Principal, Mr. Emrys Evans had spoken on *The Prospects for Peace*. Mrs. Thoday had established a home for refugees in Llanfairfechan and NWWPC members supported it throughout WW2. They also supported the Bangor Famine Relief Committee – sending food to Belgium. And Mrs. Thoday attended monthly WILPF meetings.

The NWWPC and Bangor WILPF continued to be active well into the 1960's and Dilys Pritchard who was secretary of the latter for several years, spent time at the Greenham Common Women's Peace Camp, founded in September 1981 by a group of thirty-six Welsh women: *Women for Life on Earth* and four Welsh men, from Cardiff. They crossed the Severn Bridge and walked 120 miles to the Greenham Common RAF Base near Newbury in Berkshire. Their intention was to peacefully protest about the intended siting of ninety-six American Tomahawk Cruise Missiles on British soil. When their request to speak with the Base Commander was ignored, the thirty-six women, in relays of four, chained themselves to the perimeter fence.

Subsequently they set up the women only Peace Camp, enduring appalling conditions – particularly during the winters; and later, harsh treatment by the police whenever they caused disruption or illegally entered the base; and by bailiffs sent to evict them from their camp. Many women served prison sentences but returned to the camp on their release.

In December 1982 an estimated 30-35,000 women took part in *Embrace the Base* – holding hands around the entire nine mile perimeter. The first missiles arrived in 1983. Mikhail Gorbachev and Ronald Reagan signed the Intermediate Range Nuclear Forces Treaty in December 1987. The first missiles left the base in 1989 and the last in 1991, but the Peace Camp remained for nineteen years until 2,000.

More recently, in 2014, four Welsh women: Anna Jane Evans, Sian ap Gwynfor, Awel Irene and Angharad Tomos: members of *Cymdeithas y Cymod* (Fellowship of Reconciliation) held a protest at Llanbedr Airfield, a former RAF base near Harlech, against the airfield's owner's deal with QuinetiQ to develop drones for use in warfare. They painted

dim adar angau – no death drones

on the runway. When they appeared in court at Caernarfon charged with criminal damage, the women stated that the damage was not permanent and that, as Christians, they answered to:

a higher law.

The District Judge accepted that they had acted out of their conviction, but the criminal damage was proved and they each received a six months suspended sentence and were ordered to pay £565 compensation and costs.

Peace groups continue to meet in Bangor and Anglesey; Conwy County and Wrexham.

Section 6a

Pilgrimage for Peace
Who was Who

Note: it has not been possible to trace many of the people mentioned, due to the length of time which had elapsed between the 1911 Census and the Pilgrimage, and the 1921 Census not yet being available.

North Wales Women's Peace Council

Officers:

Mrs. Edwards (Llanfairfechan) treasurer

Mrs. Silyn ROBERTS, joint-secretary, was the wife of a Welsh Methodist Minister in Blaenau Ffestiniog. He had worked as a quarryman before entering the ministry, was a poet and won the crown at the 1902 Eisteddfod. He also established the Workers Educational Association in North Wales.

During WW1 Mrs. Silyn Roberts was the North Wales Organiser for the Women's Land Army and she was the un-named woman who accused the WI of being undemocratic.

Mrs. Gwladys THODAY, joint-secretary, was the wife of David, Professor of Botany at UCNW. He was assisted in his work by Gwladys, who had herself studied Botany at Girton

College, Cambridge, and as a research fellow at Newnham College. She wrote a number of papers on botanical subjects.

During WW2 a Czech family and a Jewish family from Vienna lived in the house she had set up for refugees in Llanfairfechan. Mrs. Thoday died in 1943.

Mrs. Charlotte Price WHITE, chairman, who had been secretary of Bangor NUWSS, was an active worker in Liberal politics and education as well as the NWWPC. In 1926 she became the first woman to serve on Caernarfonshire County Council and was described as being:

> diligent, an accomplished speaker and highly respected.

She was a member of the North Wales Colleges and Bangor Local Governing Body; having been appointed chairman of the Committee of the County School for Girls, shortly before her death. She died in 1942 and her obituary said:

> By her untimely death, the city of Bangor has lost a vigorous and interesting personality.

Her family had intended her funeral to be private, but were so besieged with pleas to be allowed to attend, that the service was opened to the public and the English Presbyterian Chapel was packed. Such was the regard in which she was held that there were nearly 100 foral tributes and flags flew at half-mast throughout the city.

Speakers:

Rev. George Maitland (Temple) Lloyd DAVIES was born in 1880 in Liverpool, the son of John, a tea merchant, and

Gwen. After completing his education he entered the Bank of Liverpool and in 1908 became manager of the Wrexham branch. He then took a commission in the Royal Welch Fusiliers (Territorials). In 1913 he resigned his commission and became secretary of the Welsh Town Planning and Housing Trust. Next he took an unpaid post with the Fellowship of Reconciliation.

In 1916 Mr. Davies married Naomi Royde-Smith and they had one daughter. As a conscientious objector he was imprisoned several times during WW1. In 1923 he was elected as the Christian Pacifist MP for the University of Wales. In 1926 he was ordained as a minister in the Calvanistic Methodist Church and served in Tywyn and Maethlon until 1930. He then moved to south Wales and worked in the most poverty stricken areas, before joining a Quaker settlement in the Rhondda in 1932. In 1946 he retired to Dolwyddelan and despite failing health, continued to preach regularly. In 1949, whilst suffering from severe depression, he died in tragic circumstances.

Sir (David) Emrys EVANS was born in 1891 in Clydach, the son of Rev. Tom Valentine Evans, a Welsh Baptist minister. Emrys graduated from UCNW, Bangor, with a first-class honours degree in Latin in 1911 and Greek in 1912. After a short period teaching, he was elected Assistant Lecturer in Classics at Bangor in 1919 and Professor of Classics at Swansea in 1921.

He married Nesta Jones in 1927 and they had a son and a daughter. The same year, he returned to Bangor as Principal and remained until his retirement in 1958, when he was made a Freeman of the city. During his time as Principal he served in many other capacities both within and outside education. He was knighted in 1952 and died in 1966.

Sir Cynan Albert Evans JONES was better known as *Cynan the Bard*. He was born in 1895 in Pwllheli, the son of Richard Albert and Hannah. Richard was the proprietor of the Central Restaurant in the town. Cynan was educated at Pwllheli County School and the UCNW, Bangor, and graduated in 1916. In WW1 he joined the Welsh Student Company of the Royal Army Medical Corps serving in Salonica and France, first as an ambulance-man and then as a chaplain. Some people regard Cynan as the pre-eminent Welsh war poet, due to his poems having been written during his time serving in the RAMC.

After the war Cynan trained as a Presbyterian minister and his first appointment, in 1920, was to Penmaenmawr, where he served until 1931. He then became a tutor in the Extramural Department of the UCNW, specialising in drama and Welsh literature. Despite leaving the ministry, Cynan often conducted services and was one of the most popular non-conformist preachers of his day.

But Cynan is probably best remembered for his contribution to the National Eisteddfod, particularly for imbuing the ceremonies with a sense of drama and pageant – making them more attractive to the crowds. He held high office as Archdruid twice, but was also a keen competitor and won the crown on three occasions and the chair once. He wrote two plays and several volumes of poetry.

He married Ellen Jones and they had a son and a daughter. Ellen died in 1962. He then married Menna Merion Jones in 1963. The same year he was made a Freeman of Pwllheli. He was knighted in 1969 and died in 1970.

Mr. Elias Henry JONES was born in 1883 in Aberystwyth, the son of Sir Henry and his wife, Annie. Elias was educated at Glasgow High School and University, the University of

Grenoble, and Balliol College, Oxford, where he gained his MA. He was called to the bar, but also passed the Indian Civil Service examination and in 1905 went to serve in Burma. In 1913 he married Mair Olwen Evans.

Elias is probably best remembered for his account of a cunning escape in WW1 *The Road to Endor*, describing how he joined the Indian Army as a private soldier and was commissioned just before being taken prisoner by the Turks. He survived a 700 mile march during which, one in every seven prisoners died. He was a prisoner for three years, until he and a comrade, feigning madness, were repatriated only a fortnight before the Armistice.

Elias retired from his post as Financial Commissioner in Burma in 1922 and took up residence in Bangor, where he actively supported the movement for international peace. From 1927-1933 he was the Editor of *The Welsh Outlook*. In 1933 he was appointed Registrar of the UCNW, Bangor, and held the post until his death in 1947.

Conclusion

Not too many people have the luxury of sitting for hours on end in Archives trawling through old newspapers. But I believe that it is the information contained therein, albeit usually deferential, which brings to life the people mentioned in the main body of text.

Who can forget the description of a winter so bitter that in Amlwch, agricultural workers, fishermen and miners were unable to work for weeks on end. The provision of a Soup Kitchen where soup cost one penny for two pints to the recipients – contrasting with The Royal Welsh Yacht Club Ball at Caernarfon attended by 450 guests, with a menu which included Dressed Lobster with salad, Boar's Head and Eclaires du Chocolat, amongst numerous other delicacies.

High Days – at 3 pm on a perfect June day in **1897** 200 children each wearing a Queen Victoria's Diamond Jubilee Medal donated by Lady Gwen Neave, marched up the lawn to her home Llys Dulas, preceded by Cemaes Volunteer Band. Awaiting them, under the trees, were long tables laden with all manner of edibles and urns of tea. Grace having been sung, the children set to in earnest and soon there was not a morsel left. Sports followed, then a multitude of pretty balloons floated up into the air, their progress watched with delight by children and adult helpers alike. Before they left, Lady Gwen presented each child with a Jubilee Mug with dual portraits of Her Majesty in 1837 and 1897, and a bag containing a bun, an orange and some nuts. In the evening there was a firework display.

And holidays – Mr. and Mrs. Clegg's huge Christmas Tree delivered to the National School, lit with a hundred tapers and decorated with prizes – baskets, carriages, dolls, knives, whips, work-boxes, and other such coveted boyish and girlish property. As well as their prize, each child left with a bag containing an orange and sweets.

Weddings – Lillie Mansell-Morgan's dress of richest ivory duchesse satin, covered with old Brussels lace from her mother's wedding gown, her tulle veil fixed with three diamond stars, the gift of the bridegroom ...

and Funerals – Harry Clegg's coffin – which could not even be glimpsed due to the number of beautiful floral tributes covering it, and watched over throughout the night by relays of his tenants.

I hope that the biographies will provide readers with a colourful picture of a way of life long gone, but nonetheless, worth remembering.

Barbara Lawson-Reay.
September 2019

Acknowledgments

I wish to thank the following:

Myrddin ap Dafydd at Carreg Gwalch for his belief in this project and continued support

Eleri Owen for her imagination and skill in transforming a simple photograph into a dramatic and eye-catching cover

Mabon ap Gwynfor and family for their permission to quote from his great-grandfather, Dan Thomas' diaries

Roger Wright/Sally Davies for information concerning Isabel de Steiger.

Adrian Hughes of The Home Front Museum, Llandudno for his expertise in tracing Lieut. David Watkin Hamlen-Williams

Alan Cumming for information concerning Scottish Women's Hospitals

Angharad Rhys Williams for information concerning Dr. Helena Jones

The helpful staff at the following Archives:
Anglesey
Conwy

Denbighshire
UCNW, Bangor
National Library of Wales

Members of Gwynedd Family History Society for their painstaking and detailed research of gravestone inscriptions in churchyards throughout Gwynedd and Anglesey.

Photographic Credits:

Firstly, I wish to thank my husband, John for his patience and skill in enhancing the photographs.

I also wish to thank the following:

The National Federation of Women's Institutes Archives for permission to use the cover photograph.

Adrian Hughes of The Home Front Museum, Llandudno for bringing to my attention the photograph of Deganwy QM's Needlework Guild

Mr. & Mrs. P. Vaughan for permission to use:
    Lieut. David Watkin Hamlen-Williams
    Dr. Theophilus Richard Hamlen-Williams

Anglesey Federation of Women's Institutes for permission to use:
    Early photograph Llanfairpwll WI
    Col. Hon. Richard Stapleton-Cotton, Tinker
    Hon. Mrs. Jane Stapleton-Cotton
    Mrs. W.E. Jones
    Mrs. Madge Watt

John Cowell for permission to use:
    A fête marquee
    Menai Bridge Lawn Tennis Club
    A greeting arch
    Amlwch Soup Kitchen organisers

Archives and Special Collections, Bangor University for permission to use:
    The North Wales Peace Pilgrimage at Conway
    The North Wales Peace Pilgrimage at Rhyl.

Bibliography

Local Newspapers:
Brecon & Radnor Express
Cambria Daily Leader
Cambrian News
Chester Courant
Denbighshire Free Press
Evening Express
Flintshire Observer
Llangollen Advertiser
North Wales Chronicle
North Wales Express
Rhyl Journal
Western Mail
Wrexham Advertiser
Wrexham Leader
https://newspapers.library.wales
    (Welsh Newspapers Online-Home)

1911 Census   1901 Census

Section 1, 1a, 1b: Suffrage activities in North East Wales:
Mrs. Brown is a Man and Brother: Women in Merseyside's Political Organisations – Krista Cowman
The Women's Suffrage Movement – Elizabeth Crawford
The Women's Suffrage Movement in Britain and Ireland – Elizabeth Crawford
The Women's Suffrage Movement in Wales – Ryland Wallace

Section 2, 2a: Llangollen NUWSS Minute Book and Any Other Business

Llangollen NUWSS Minute Book (National Library of Wales)

An Illustrated History of Llangollen – Gordon Sherratt

Section 3, 3a: The Welsh Hospital, Netley, Southampton

Spike Island – Philip Hoare

www.netley-military-cemetery.co.uk

Section 4, 4a: Scottish Women's Hospitals for service abroad

www.nationalarchives.gov.uk (SWH)

Section 5, 5a: Llanfairpwll Women's Institute

A Grain of Mustard Seed – Constance Davies

A Force to be Reckoned With – Jane Robinson

The WI – A Century in the Making – Mavis Curtis

Memorial Inscriptions of the Church of St. Mary, Llanfairpwll – Gwynedd Family History Society

Section 6, 6a: Pilgrimage for Peace

Peace Pilgrimage Scrapbook compiled by Gwladys Thoday – (UCNW Archives)

Bibliography/primary sources

Local Newspapers:
Brecon & Radnor Express
Cambria Daily Leader
Cambrian News
Chester Courant
Denbighshire Free Press
Evening Express
Flintshire Observer
Llangollen Advertiser
North Wales Chronicle
North Wales Express
Rhyl Journal
Western Mail
Wrexham Advertiser
Wrexham Leader
https://newspapers.library.wales (Welsh Newspapers Online-Home)

Section 1 Suffrage Activities in North-East Wales:
Newspapers as indicated in text
Papers of J. Williams, Bryn Siriol, Stanley Road, Ponciau.
Reminiscences of J.W. Williams:
DD/DM/934/2 Proposed Conservative meeting at Johnstown with Suffragette Margaret MacDougall as speaker – Denbighshire Archives
DD/DN/934/2 Political Cockpit on Ponkey Banks and Suffragette Meeting at Wrexham with Christabel Pankhurst as speaker – Denbighshire Archives
Family Diaries often offer a treasured window into the past and the diary of Dan Thomas is no exception – *Wrexham Leader* – 29 October 2014
The Women's Suffrage Movement in Wales – Ryland Wallace
Section 1a: Denbigh, Ruthin and Wrexham NUWSS Members:
The Women's Suffrage Movement – Elizabeth Crawford

Section 1b Visiting Suffragists, Suffragettes and Supporters:
Mrs. Brown is a Man and Brother: Women in Merseyside's Political Organisations – Krista Cowman
The Women's Suffrage Movement – Elizabeth Crawford
The Women's Suffrage Movement in Britain and Ireland – Elizabeth Crawford
https://newspapers.library.wales
   (Welsh Newspapers Online-Home)

Section 2 Llangollen NUWSS Minute Book and Any Other Business
Llangollen NUWSS Minute Book – The National Library of Wales
Section 2a Llangollen NUWSS Members:
1911 Census
1901 Census
The Llangollen Advertiser
An Illustrated History of Llangollen – Gordon Sherratt
The Women's Suffrage Movement – Elizabeth Crawford
www.quakersintheworld.org (Elsie Cadbury)
www.telegraph.co.uk Lifestyle Foodand drink Cadbury heritage
www.russellcroft.net blog tag=edith-eskrigge
www.wrightanddavid.co.uk ISABELART (Isabel de Steiger)
https://newspapers.library.wales (Welsh Newspapers Online-Home)

Section 3 The Welsh Hospital, Netley, Southampton:
Palace of Pain: Netley – Philip Hoare – *The Guardian* 21 August 2014
Spike Island – Philip Hoare
www.netley-military-cemetery.co.uk
Section 3a:The Welsh Hospital Patients and Patrons:
https://pure.aber.ac.uk portal files A plentiful crop of cripples (Mr. J.J. Stubbs)
www.revolvy.com page Violet-Mond-Baroness-Melchett
https://biography.wales article s2-THOM-JAM-1867 (Sir William James Thomas)
https://newspapers.library.wales (Welsh Newspapers Online-Home)

Section 4 Scottish Women's Hospitals or service abroad:
www.nationalarchives.gov.uk
Section 4a Scottish Women's Hospitals Staff:
Votes for Women – North Wales Suffragist's Campaign for the Vote 1907-1914 – Barbara Lawson-Reay
https://www.rcpe.ac.uk heritage college history elsieinglis
www.llangammarchhistory.co.uk (Dr. Mary Phillips)

Section 5 Llanfairpwll Women's Institute:
A Grain of Mustard Seed – Constance Davies
A Force to be Reckoned With – Jane Robinson
The WI – A Century in the Making – Mavis Curtis
https://newspapers.library.wales (Welsh Newspapers Online-Home)
Section 5a Llanfairpwll Women's Institute Members 1915-1921:
1911 Census
1901 Census
Memorial Inscriptions of the Church of St. Mary, Llanfairpwll – Gwynedd Family History Society
https://newspapers.library.wales (Welsh Newspapers Online-Home)

Section 6 Pilgrimage for Peace:
Peace Pilgrimage Scrapbook compiled by Gwladys Thoday – University of Bangor Archives
https://armingallsides.org.uk case_studies at-the-front-of-the-march
https://www.bbc.co.ukl news uk-wales-north-wet-wales 37429991 (March through Caernarfon)
Section 6a Officers and Committee Members: North Wales Women's Peace Council:
1911 Census
https://newspapers.library.wales (Welsh Newspapers Online-Home)

Index

Double-barrelled Surnames will be found under the second name. First name in brackets denotes they were known by the following name.
Bold page numbers denote photographs
Supporters & Members of Llangollen NUWSS & Llanfairpwll WI are listed in Section 2a & Section 5a respectively. Only the names of those who have biographical details in addition to those obtained from the Census & Burial Records, are included in this Index.

Abbreviations:
AOS: Agricultural Organisation Society
ASL: Anti-Suffrage League
BOAF: Board of Agriculture & Fisheries
(C'fon) Caernarfon
ILP: Independent Labour Party
(Ll NUWSS) Llangollen National Union Women's Suffrage Societies: law-abiding Suffragists
(Ll'pwll) Llanfairpwll
(Ll'pwll WI) Llanfairpwll WI
(MB) Menai Bridge
NUWSS: National Union Women's Suffrage Societies
(P) Peace
POWs: Prisoners of War
QM's: Queen Mary's Needlework Guild
SWH: Scottish Women's Hospitals
WEA: Worker's Educational Association
WFL: Women's Freedom League
(WH): Welsh Hospital, Netley, Southampton
(W'ham) Wrexham
WILPF: Women's International League for Peace & Freedom
WLWC&NW: West Lancashire, West Cheshire & North Wales Federation NUWSS
WSPU: Women's Social & Political Union: militant Suffragettes

GEE, Mrs. Susannah (Denbigh) 30
Geneva Disarmament Conference 236
Lloyd **GEORGE**, Mr. David, MP 33,35,44,48,53,74,180
Lloyd **GEORGE**, Mrs. Margaret 106,180
Lloyd **GEORGE**, Miss Megan 106
GILL, Miss Helga (NUWSS) 25,26,27,41
GIMINGHAM, Miss C. (NUWSS) 29,30,31,41-42
GLADSTONE Miss Helen 33
GLADSTONE Mr. William Ewart 33,161
GOODWIN, Nurse Winifred (NUWSS/SWH)
60,62,63,85,113
GOODWIN, Miss 135,137
Ormesby-**GORE**, Mr. William MP 32
Herr **GOTLIEB's** Band 171
Mrs. **GOUGH's** Orchestra 180
GRAHAM, Mrs. (Wirral-P) 228,229
Great Western Railway 84
Greenham Common Women's Peace Camp 239
Grenadier Guards, Band of 174
GREY, Sir Edward 43
Groeslon (P) 224
Gwalchmai Aerodrome/Isolation Hospital 140
Gwynedd Ladies'Art Society 215
Gyffin (P) 224

HADDOW, Miss Grace (WI) 121
Harlech 178; (P) 240
HARLEY, (Mrs. Katherine) Memorial Loan Fund (SWH)
75,77,78
Harper-Adams Agricultural College 184
HARRIS, Mr. John Nugent (AOS) 123,143,147,186
HARRIS, Mrs. Nugent (AOS/WI) 128,141
HARROD's 100
Hawarden 33
HENLEY, Mr. 215
HILL, Mrs. Margaret (Llangollen) 19
Hindu cremation (WH) 103
HODGSON, Mr. (Ruthin) 20
Holloway 38,45
Holyhead 184

(WH) 106
Mr. **RICHARDSON's** Band (Liverpool) 209,211
ROBERTS, Mr. E.J. (Denbigh) 30
ROBERTS, Sir Herbert MP 69,70,72,74,75,76
ROBERTS, Mrs. Silyn (P) 223,227,233,235,242
Ro-wen (P) 224
Royal Victoria Military Hospital (Southampton) 96,97
Royal Welch Fusiliers 162,197
RSPCA 163,180,196,197,198
Ruabon 13,25,26
RUDOLPH, Rev. E. de M. (Waifs & Strays) 178
Ruthin 20,31,32

SALISBURY, Lord 205,206
Cobden-**SANDERSON**, Mrs. Anne (WSPU/WFL) 25,53-54,
SCHWIMMER, Rosika (P) 62
SEARELL, Mr. R.B. (Denbigh) 27
Smallpox 171
Assheton-SMITH, Mr. George William Duff (Faenol) 177,178-179,193,205
Assheton-**SMITH**, Mrs. George (Faenol) 177,178
Assheton-**SMITH**, Mr. Thomas 178
Hunter-**SMITH**, Mrs. 129
SMITH, Mr. James (Coastguard) 210
Gladstone-**SOLOMON**, Mrs. (ASL) 35
SPENCER, Miss Mildred (NUWSS) 55,72
Sphagnum Moss dressings 100/**100**
St. Asaph 20,178
St. David's Day 106 (WH), 150 (Ll WI)
St. Dunstan's 138
St. Kitts (Leeward Islands) 192
St. Paul's altar cloth (WH) 104
STALYBRASS, Mrs. Greville (NUWSS) 36
John **STANLEY's** Butcher's shop **195**
de **STEIGER**, Madame Isabel(le) (Ll. NUWSS) 56,64,65,84,89-91
STEWART, Miss Beatrice (Jnr.) (Ll NUWSS) 21,22,23, 36,55,56,57,58,59, 60,63,64,65,66,67,69,70,71,72,74,75,76,77, 78,79,80,81,84
STEWART, Miss Beatrice (Snr.) (Ll NUWSS) 78,79,80,87,91-92,

By the same author:

**The history of the campaign in North Wales
to secure votes for women 1907-1914**

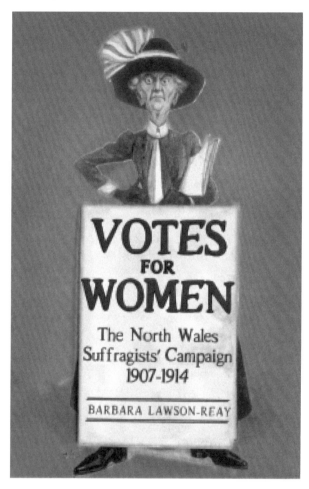

£8.50
Gwasg Carreg Gwalch